E S T A T E   P U B L I

SOUTHEND-ON-
CANVEY · SOUTH BENFLEET · LEIGH
ROCHFORD · WESTCLIFF-ON-SEA ·

G000295962

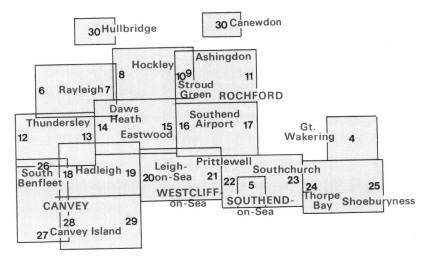

30 Hullbridge	30 Canewdon

Hockley 8   Ashingdon 10 9   11
6   Rayleigh 7   Stroud Green   ROCHFORD
Daws Heath
Thundersley 14   15 16 Southend Airport 17   Gt. Wakering 4
12   13   Eastwood
26
South Benfleet 18 Hadleigh 19   Leigh-on-Sea 20 Prittlewell 21   Southchurch 23
CANVEY   22 5   Thorpe Bay 24   25
WESTCLIFF-on-Sea   SOUTHEND-on-Sea   Shoeburyness
28   29
27 Canvey Island

ROAD MAP   pages 2-3
SOUTHEND ENLARGED CENTRE page 5
INDEX TO STREETS   page 31

Every effort has been made to verify the accuracy of information in this book but the publishers cannot accept responsibility for expense or loss caused by any error or omission. Information that will be of assistance to the user of the maps will be welcomed.

The representation of a road, track or footpath on the maps in this atlas is no evidence of the existence of a right of way.

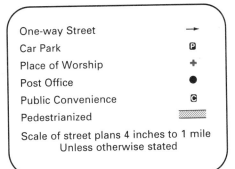

One-way Street   →
Car Park   P
Place of Worship   +
Post Office   ●
Public Convenience   C
Pedestrianized

Scale of street plans 4 inches to 1 mile
Unless otherwise stated

Street plans prepared and published by ESTATE PUBLICATIONS, Bridewell House, TENTERDEN, KENT, and based upon the ORDNANCE SURVEY maps with the sanction of the Controller of H. M. Stationery Office.

The publishers acknowledge the co-operation of Southend-on-Sea, Castle Point and Rochford District Councils in the preparation of these maps.

© Estate Publications 078 L   ISBN 0 86084 748 9

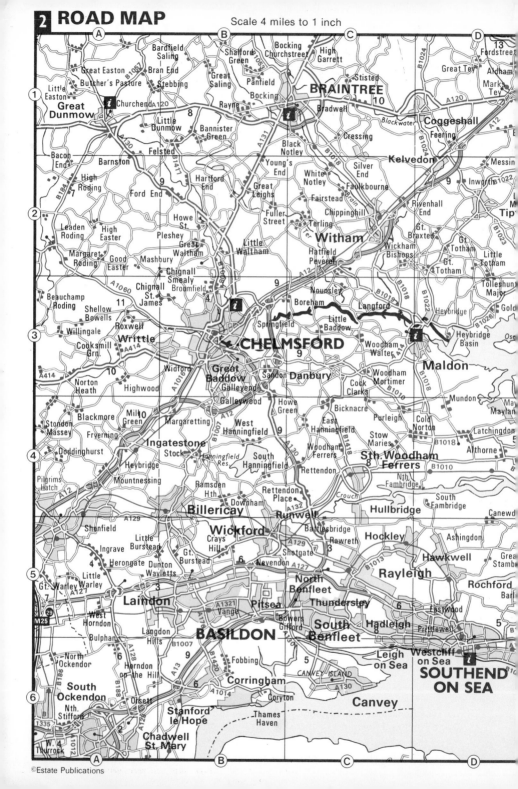

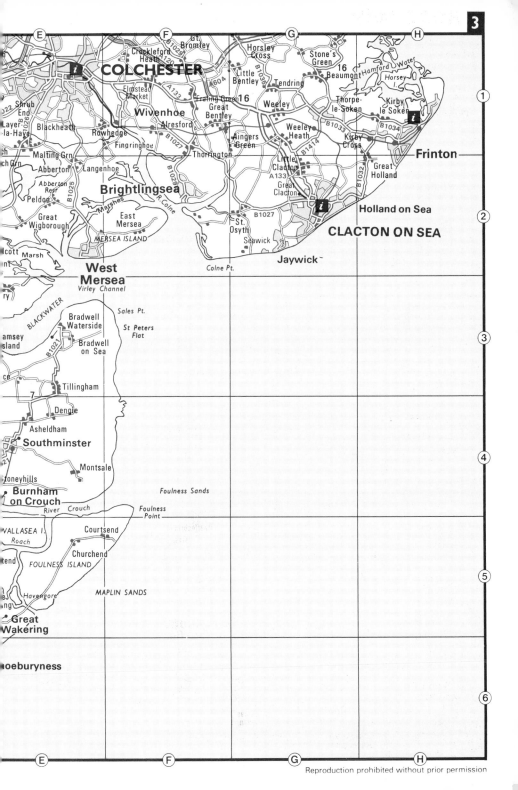

3

E · F · G · H

Gt Bromley
Crockleford Heath
COLCHESTER ⓘ
Elmstead Market
A133
Wivenhoe
Alresford
Shrub End
Blackheath
Rowhedge
Layer-de-la-Haye
Fingringhoe
Malting Grn
Abberton
Langenhoe
Abberton Reservoir
Peldon
Great Wigborough
East Mersea
Brightlingsea
Marshes
R.Colne
MERSEA ISLAND
West Mersea
Virley Channel

Horsley Cross
Little Bentley
Frating Green 16
Great Bentley
Aingers Green
Thorrington
Tendring
Weeley
Weeley Heath
Little Clacton
A133
Great Clacton
St. Osyth
Seawick
B1027
Jaywick
Colne Pt.

Stone's Green 16
Beaumont
Hamford Water
Horsey I.
Thorpe-le-Soken
Kirby le Soken ⓘ
B1033
Kirby Cross
B1034
Frinton
Great Holland
ⓘ
Holland on Sea
CLACTON ON SEA

BLACKWATER
Bradwell Waterside
Sales Pt.
St Peters Flat
Bradwell on Sea
B1021
amsey Island
Tillingham
7
Dengie
Asheldham
Southminster
Montsale
toneyhills
Burnham on Crouch
River Crouch
Foulness Sands
Foulness Point
WALLASEA I.
Roach
end
Courtsend
Churchend
FOULNESS ISLAND
Havengore
ng
Great Wakering
MAPLIN SANDS
oeburyness

1
2
3
4
5
6

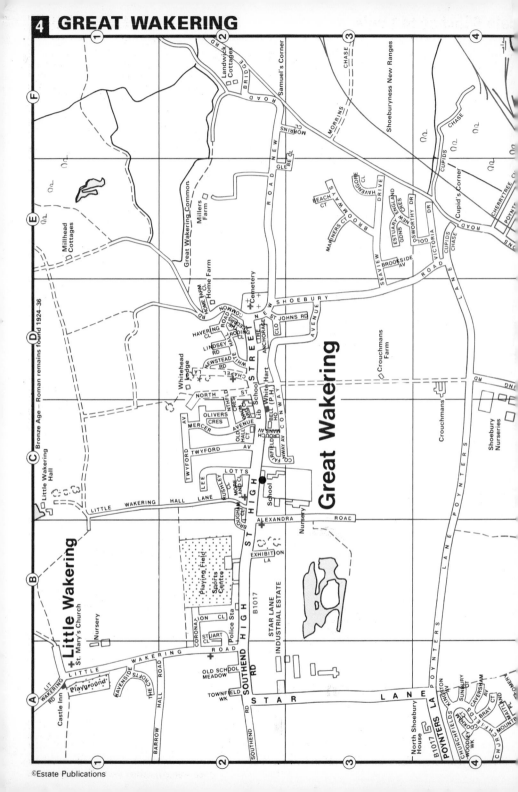

Great Wakering

Little Wakering

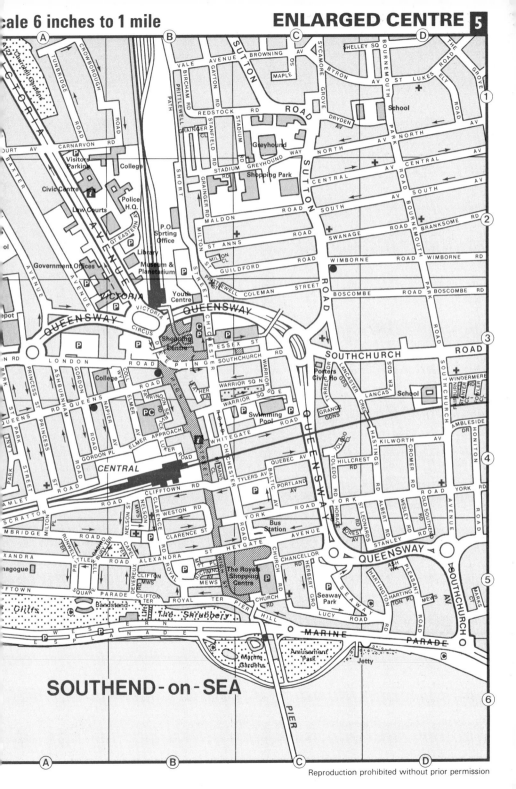

Chichester Hall

LONDON ROAD

A129

LONDON ROAD

Carpenters' Arms (P.H.)

Garage

CHELMSFORD RD

A130

CHELMSFORD RD

BEKE HALL CHASE

ST JOHNS DR

BEKE HALL CHASE SOUTH

RAYLEIGH SPUR ROAD

A130

A127

RAWRETH INDUSTRIAL ESTATE

Eastern Electricity Board Offices

CHEAPSIDE
MARMADUKE AV
BOSTON AV
SALEM
NEWPORT CT
BENFLEET CT
VACHE
FIRMEAD
SWEYNE CL
VICTORIA
SPRINGFLD CT
HARTFORD CT
WAYNE CRES

R.C. School

Playing Field

LITTLE WHEATLEY CHASE
LOUIS DR W
LOUIS DR
LEONARD DR
RONALD DR
ALEXANDRIA DRIVE
LOUIS DR E
VICTORIA ROAD
WALTHAM RD

HADDON
WHEATLEY
GOSFIELD CL
NEWSUM GN
BARDFIELD
WILLINGALE AV
COLD HANGER CL
TILLINGHAM WAY
FYFIELD PATH
TENDRING AV
FIELD
PURLE

LANGHAM DR
BROOM FLD AV
HANNINGFIELD
STOCK
HAVENGORE
WETHERSFIELD CL
LATCHINGDON
KETTENDON
RETTENDON CL
FALCON CL
HATFIELD

AIDHAM GDNS
BOXFORD
OAKLEY AV
ASHFIELD
OAKLEY AV
DRIVE
LANGHAM DR
LINDSEY
STREET
BROMLEY
DENHAM VALE
TOLSEY CL

KESTREL C
KINGFISH
CLIFTON
ROD

SOUTHEND ROAD

RAYLEIGH SPUR ROAD

Lychgate Farm

IND EST

FANE

BURCHES

ROAD

CONISTON ROAD

Caversham Farm

Great Burches Farm

ARTERIAL

Kingley Wood

Playing Field

GT
WESTVIEW DR
WESTERN ROAD
WHE

Gr
Whe

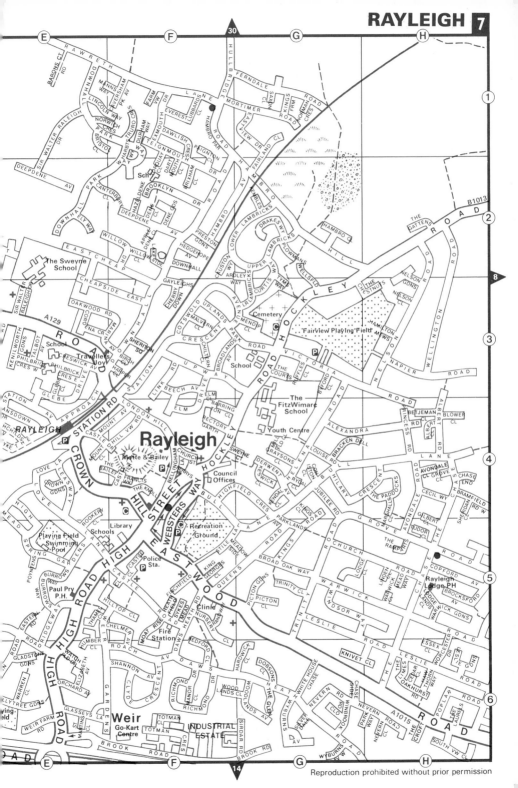

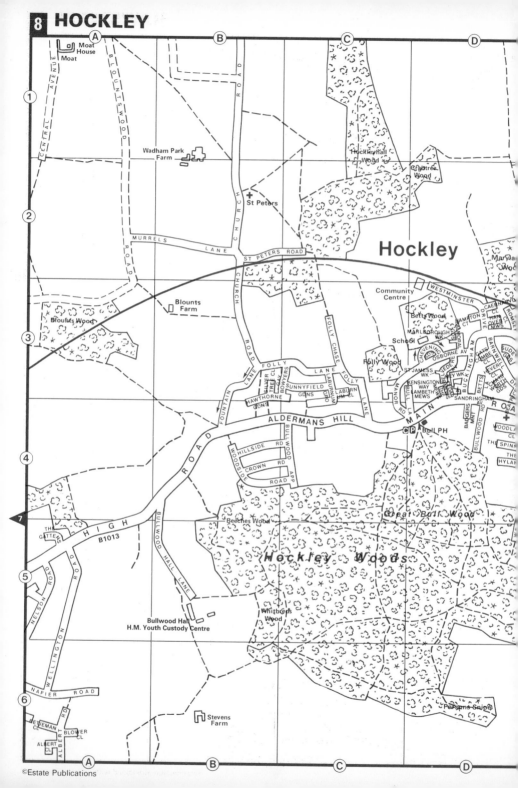

Hockley

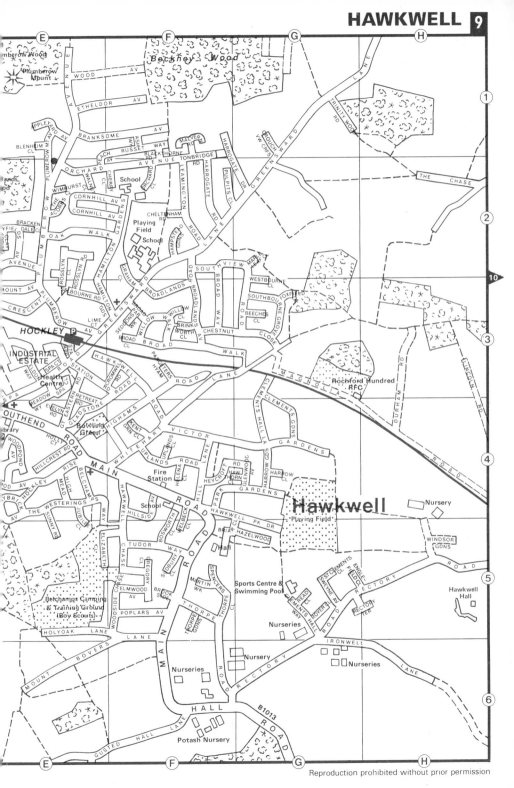

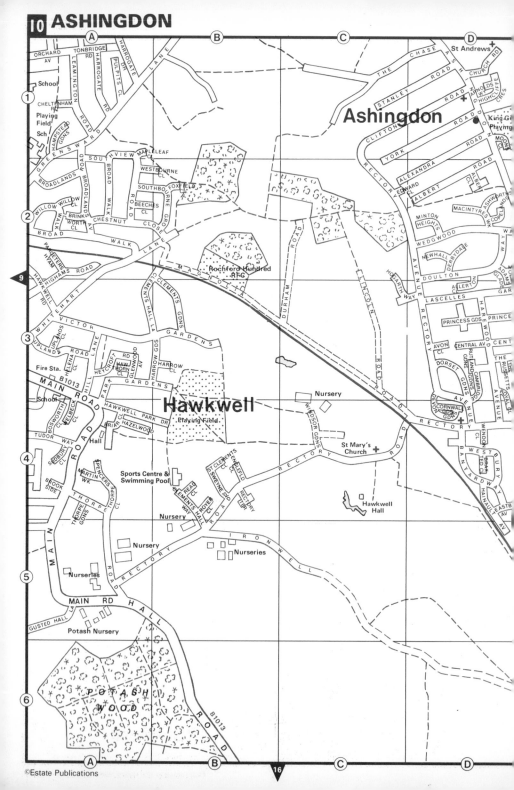

Rochford

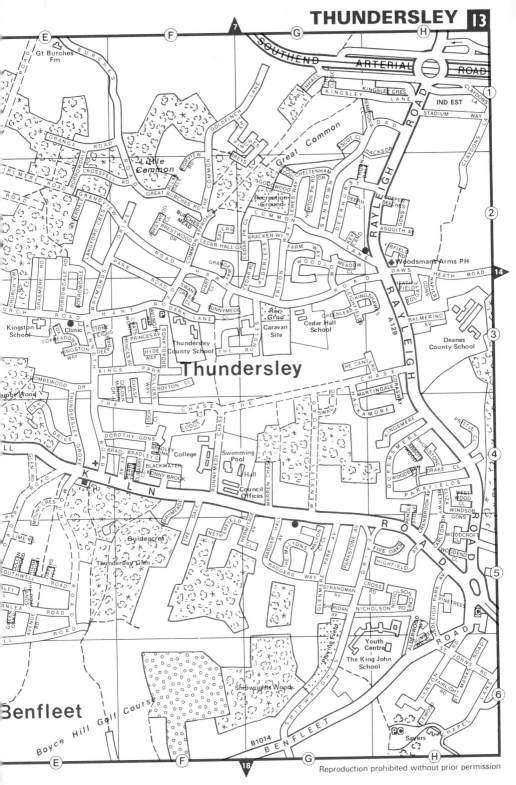

Thundersley

Benfleet

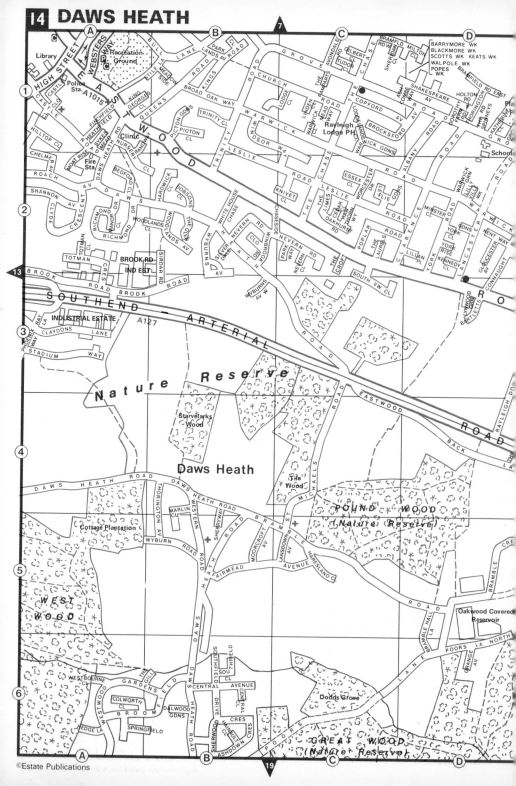

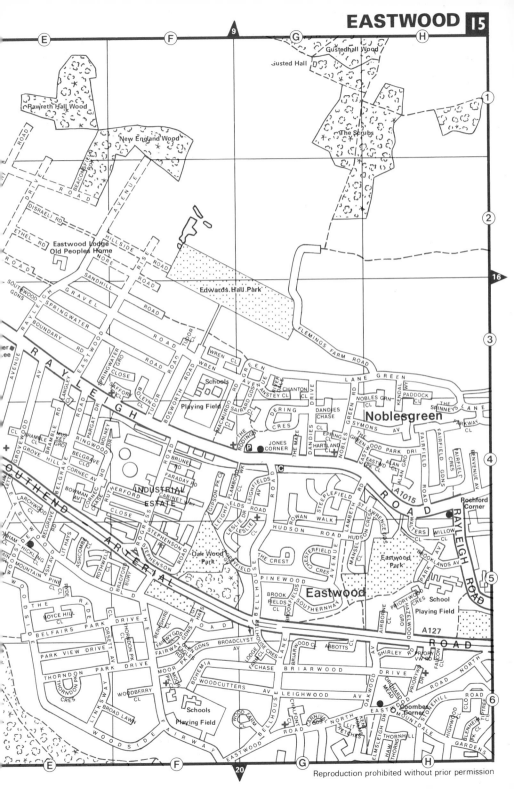

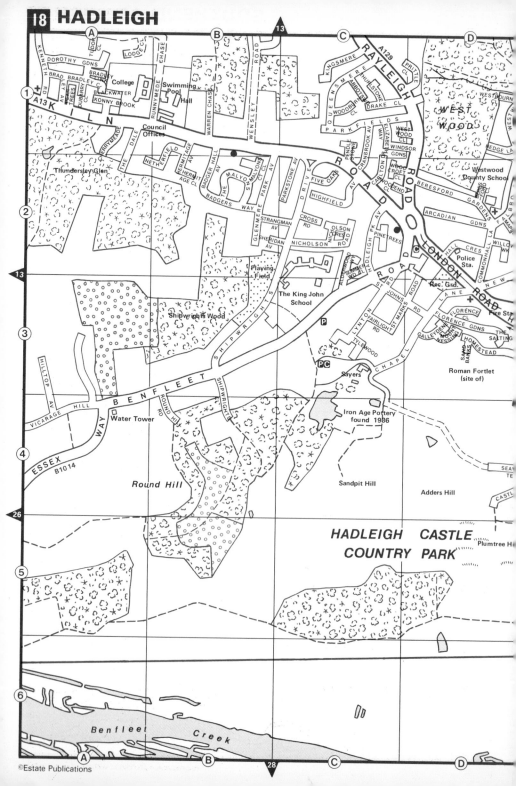

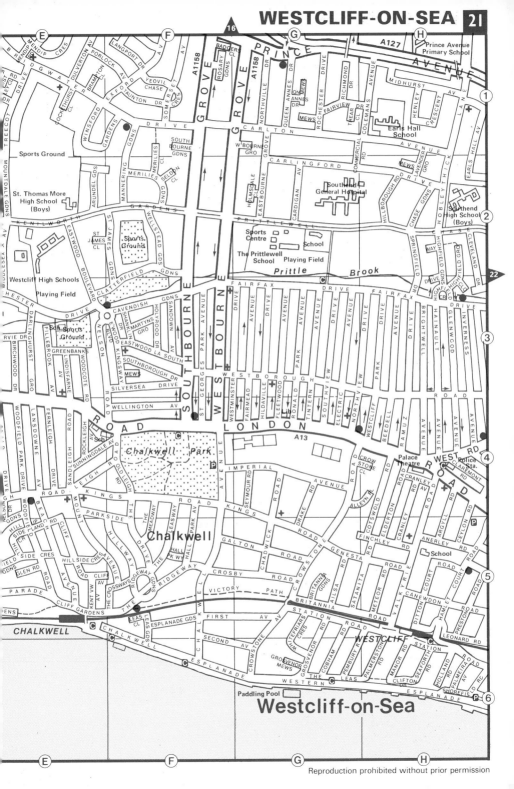

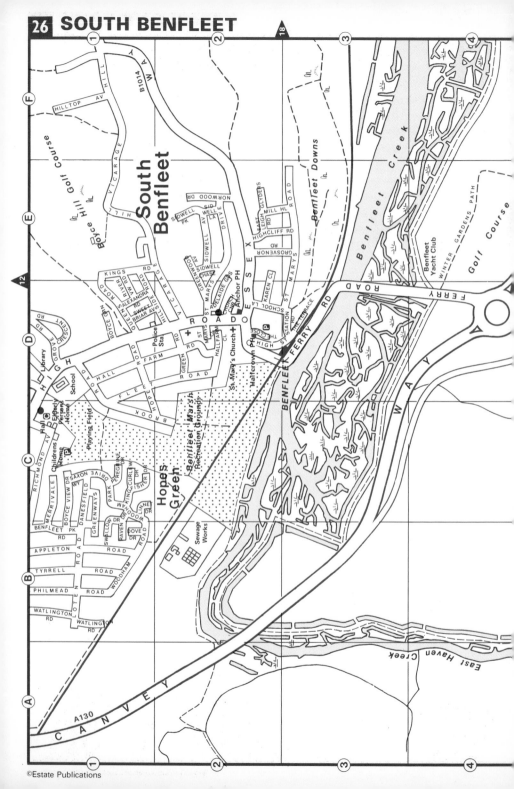

South Benfleet

Boyce Hill Golf Course

Benfleet Downs

Benfleet Creek

Benfleet Yacht Club

WINTER GARDENS PATH

Golf Course

HILLTOP AV

B1014 A WAY

VICARAGE HILL

NORWOOD DR

SIDWELL PK

SID WELL LA

SIDWELL AV

GREENWOOD

SIDWELL CHASE

ADELAIDE GDS

EAST

HIGHCLIFF RD

GROSVENOR RD

LEIGH MILL HL

GLYDERS RD

KAREN CL

ST MARYS

SCHOOL LA

ST MARYS

THE TERRACE

THE CLOSE

HIGH ST

STATION RD

KINGS ROAD

S'ALEXANDRA RD

QUEEN RIVER RW RD

SWEET BRIAR AV

BOYCE ROAD

ROAD

ST MARYS GREEN

VICARAGE

HILLSIDE

R O S T R O A D

E S S E X

BENFLEET FERRY RD

FERRY ROAD

WAY

RD

RD

HIGH GROVE CRESCENT

Library

School

RICHMOND AV

Hall

Elderly Persons Home

Childrens Home

Police Sta.

ST MARYS RD

GREEN RD

HALL FARM RD

FLEET ROAD

HOPE RD

HALL ROAD

FARM ROAD

BROOK

Playing Field

St. Mary's Church

Halfcrown PH

Anchor PH

Benfleet Marsh

Recreation Grounds

Hopes Green

MERRIVALE

BOYCE VIEW DR

DANESFIELD

GREENWAYS

SAXON DRIVE

PARK

PEREGRINE

KINGFISHER DR

CURLEW

SWALLOW DR

RAVEN DR

DOVE DR

WIDGEON

LANE

Sewage Works

BENFLEET PK RD

APPLETON ROAD

ROAD

TYRRELL ROAD

PHILMEAD ROAD

WATLINGTON RD

WATLINGTON RD

WOODHAM ROAD

OTTEN

CANVEY WAY

A130

East Haven Creek

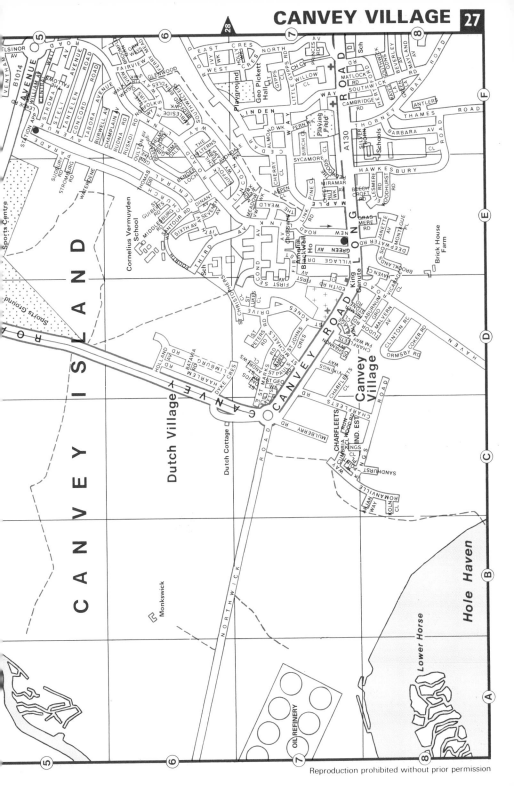

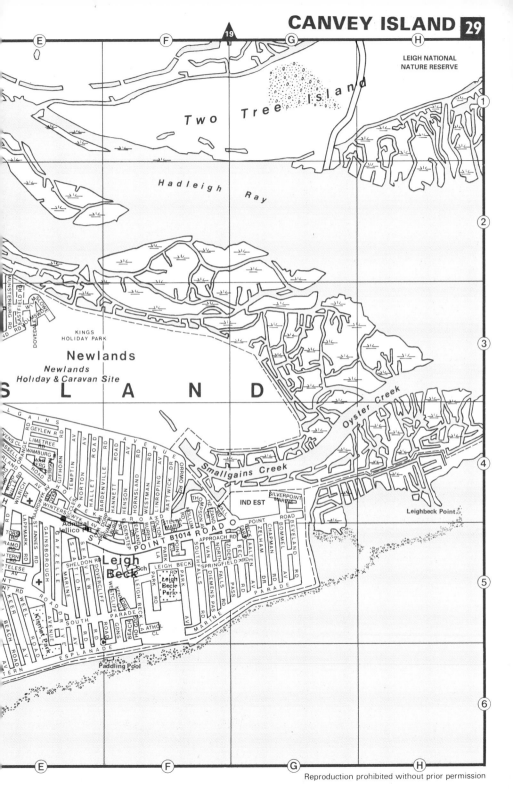

LEIGH NATIONAL
NATURE RESERVE

Two Tree Island

Hadleigh Ray

KINGS
HOLIDAY PARK

Newlands
Newlands
Holiday & Caravan Site

S L A N D

Oyster Creek

Smallgains Creek

IND EST

SILVERPOINT
MARINE

Leighbeck Point

POINT ROAD B1014

Leigh Beck

Leigh
Beck
Park

Kismet Park

Paddling Pool

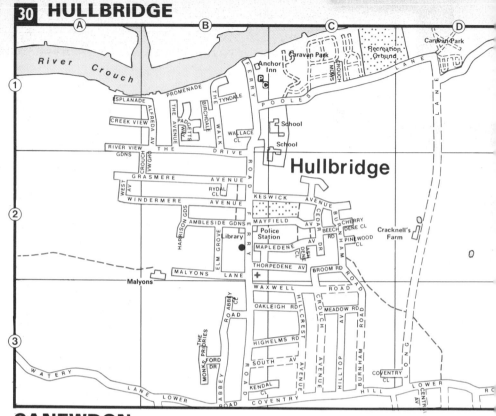

CANEWDON

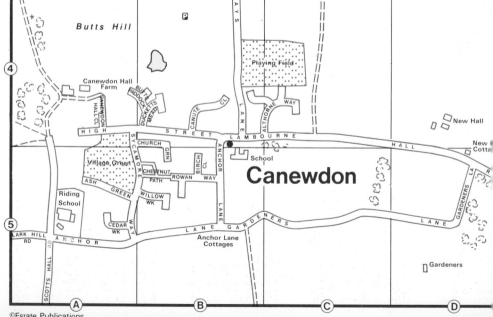

ndex includes some names for
h there is insufficient space on
aps. These names are preceded
* and are followed by the nearest
ning thoroughfare.

SOUTHEND

Street	Ref.	Street	Ref.	Street	Ref.	Street	Ref.
Brandenburg Rd. SS8	28 D2	Burdett Rd. SS1	23 E6	Cedar Park Clo. SS7	13 G2	Church Clo. SS8	2?
Branksome Av. SS5	9 E1	Buren Av. SS8	29 F5	Cedar Rd. SS8	28 A4	Church Cnr. SS7	2?
Branksome Rd. SS2	5 D2	Burfield Clo. SS9	16 A4	Cedar Rd. SS7	13 G3	Church Hill. SS9	2?
Branscombe Gdns. SS1	24 B2	Burfield Rd. SS9	16 A4	Central Av. SS5	8 A1	Church Par. SS8	2?
Branscombe Sq. SS1	24 B2	Burges Clo. SS1	24 B5	Central Av. SS4	10 D3	Church Rd. SS4	1?
Branscombe Walk. SS1	24 B2	Burges Rd. SS1	24 A4	Central Av. SS8	28 A2	Church Rd, Hadleigh. SS7	1?
Braxted Clo. SS4	10 D4	Burges Ter. SS1	23 H6	Central Av. SS7	19 E1	Church Rd. SS5	
Bray Ct. SS3	25 E1	Burleigh Sq. SS1	24 B3	Central Av. SS2	5 C2	Church Rd. SS6	
Brays La. SS4	11 E3	Burlescoombe Clo. SS1	24 A2	Central Clo. SS7	19 E1	Church Rd. SS1	
Bread and Cheese Hill. SS7	12 D3	Burlescoombe Leas. SS1	24 B2	Central Wall. SS8	28 A2	Church Rd. SS3	2?
Brendon Way. SS9	16 B5	Burlescoombe Rd. SS1	24 A2	Central Wall Path. SS8	28 A2	Church Rd Thundersley. SS7	?
Brettenham Dri. SS1	23 G5	Burlington Gdns. SS7	19 F2	Central Wall Rd. SS8	28 C2	Church St. SS6	?
Brewster Clo. SS8	28 B4	Burnaby Rd. SS1	23 E6	Centurion Clo. SS3	25 F2	Church View Rd. SS7	?
Briar Clo. SS5	9 F5	Burnham Rd. SS9	20 B3	Ceylon Rd. SS0	22 A4	Church Way. SS7	?
Briarswood. SS8	28 A2	Burnside. SS8	28 B3	Chadacre Rd. SS1	24 B2	Churchfields. SS3	2?
Briarwood Clo. SS9	15 G6	Burr Hill Chase. SS2	22 A1	Chadwick Rd. SS0	21 G5	Clare Rd. SS7	?
Briarwood Dri. SS9	15 G6	Burrows Way. SS6	7 E5	Chaffinch Clo. SS3	25 E2	Claremont Rd. SS0	?
Brickfields Way. SS4	17 G2	Burwell Av. SS8	28 A2	Chaingate Av. SS2	23 G2	Clarence Clo. SS7	?
Bridge Clo. SS3	24 D3	Butterys. SS1	23 G4	Chalfont Clo. SS9	20 C1	Clarence Rd. SS6	?
Bridgewater Dri. SS0	21 E1	Butts Rd. SS3	25 H2	Chalk Rd. SS8	28 B1	Clarence Rd. SS7	1?
Brighten Rd. SS0	22 B4	Buxton Av. SS9	19 G3	Chalkwell Av. SS0	21 F6	Clarence Rd. SS1	?
Brighton Av. SS1	23 F4	Buxton Clo. SS9	19 G3	Chalkwell Esplanade. SS0	21 F5	Clarence Rd Nth. SS7	1?
Brightwell Av. SS0	21 H3	Buxton Sq. SS9	19 H3	Chalkwell Park Dri. SS9	20 D4	Clarence St. SS1	?
Brindles. SS8	28 A3	Buyl Av. SS8	28 C2	Challacombe. SS1	24 C2	Clarendon Rd. SS8	2?
Brinkworth Clo. SS5	9 F3	Byfield. SS9	16 A3	Chamberlain Av. SS8	28 D4	Claters Clo. SS2	2?
Bristol Clo. SS6	7 E1	Byford Clo. SS6	7 G3	Champlain Av. SS8	28 A2	Clatterfield Gdns. SS0	2?
Bristol Rd. SS2	17 E4	Byrne Dri. SS2	17 E5	Chancel Clo. SS7	12 C3	Claybrick Av. SS5	
Britannia Gdns. SS0	21 G5	Byron Av. SS2	5 C1	Chancellor Rd. SS1	5 C5	Claydons La. SS6	1?
Britannia Rd. SS0	21 G5	Byron Clo. SS8	28 D3	Chandlers. SS2	17 G5	Clayspring Clo. SS5	
Brixham Clo. SS6	7 F2			Chandlers Way. SS2	17 G5	Clements Gdns. SS5	?
Broad Clo. SS5	9 F3	Cabinet Way. SS9	15 F4	Chandos Parade. SS7	19 G3	Clements Hall La. SS5	?
Broad Lawn. SS9	20 A1	Caernarvon Clo. SS5	8 D3	Chanton Clo. SS9	15 G3	Clements Hall Way. SS5	?
Broad Oak Way. SS6	7 G5	Cambridge Gdns. SS4	10 D3	Chapel La. SS7	18 C3	Cleveland Dri. SS0	2?
Broad Parade. SS5	9 F3	Cambridge Rd. SS8	28 A5	Chapel Rd. SS3	25 E5	Cleveland Rd. SS8	2
Broad Way. SS5	9 F3	Cambridge Rd. SS1	5 A5	Chapman Rd. SS8	29 G5	Clieveden Rd. SS1	2
Broadclyst Av. SS9	15 F6	Cameron Clo. SS9	20 A3	Chapmans Clo. SS9	19 H4	Cliff Av. SS9	2
Broadclyst Clo. SS1	24 A2	Camper Mews. SS1	23 F6	Chapmans Walk. SS9	19 H4	Cliff Av. SS0	2
Broadclyst Gdns. SS1	24 A2	Camper Rd. SS1	23 F6	Charfleets Clo. SS8	27 D7	Cliff Gdns. SS0	
Broadlands. SS7	13 F3	Campfield Rd. SS3	25 E4	Charfleets Farm Way. SS8	27 D7	Cliff Par. SS9	2?
Broadlands Av. SS5	10 A2	Candlemakers. SS2	17 G5	Charfleets Ind Est. SS8	27 C7	Cliff Rd. SS9	2
Broadlands Av. SS6	7 F3	Canewdon Rd. SS0	22 A4	Charfleets Rd. SS8	27 D7	Cliffsea Gro. SS9	2?
Broadlands Rd. SS5	9 F3	Canewdon Vw Rd. SS4	11 E2	Charles Clo. SS7	16 B5	Clifftown Par. SS1	?
Broadway. SS9	20 D5	Canonsleigh Cres. SS9	20 D4	Chase Clo. SS7	13 F3	Clifftown Rd. SS1	
Broadway West. SS9	20 C5	Canterbury Av. SS2	23 F1	Chase End. SS6	7 H4	Clifton Av. SS7	1?
Brocksford Av. SS6	7 H5	Canterbury Clo. SS6	7 E2	Chase Gdns. SS0	21 H2	Clifton Clo. SS7	1?
Bromley Mews. SS6	6 C4	Canvey Rd. SS8	27 D7	Chase Rd. SS1	23 E4	Clifton Dri. SS0	2?
Bronte Mews. SS2	22 D2	Canvey Rd. SS9	20 A4	Chase Side. SS6	7 G6	Clifton Mews. SS1	?
Brook Clo. SS4	17 G2	Canvey Way. SS7	12 A6	Chatsworth. SS7	13 F3	Clifton Rd. SS4	1?
Brook Rd. SS6	7 F6	Capadocia St. SS3	23 G6	Chatsworth Gdns. SS5	8 D3	Clifton Rd. SS8	2?
Brook Rd. SS7	26 C2	Capel Ter. SS1	5 B5	Cheapside East. SS6	7 E3	Clifton Ter. SS1	?
Brook Rd Ind Est. SS6	14 A2	Cardigan Av. SS0	21 G2	Cheapside West. SS6	6 D2	Clifton Way. SS7	1?
Brookfields. SS9	15 G5	Carisbrooke Rd. SS0	22 A3	Cheddar Av. SS0	16 B5	Climmen Rd. SS8	2?
Brookfields Clo. SS9	15 G5	Carlingford Dri. SS0	21 G2	Chedington. SS3	24 C2	Clinton Rd. SS8	27
Brooklands Av. SS9	15 H5	Carlton Av. SS0	21 G1	Cheldon Barton. SS1	24 C2	Clova Rd. SS9	2?
Brooklands Sq. SS9	27 E8	Carlton Dri. SS9	21 E4	Chelmer Av. SS6	7 F5	Cluny Sq. SS2	2?
Brooklyn Dri. SS6	7 F2	Carlton Dri. SS7	13 H5	Chelmer Way. SS3	24 D4	Clyde Cres. SS6	
Brookside. SS8	28 B2	Carmania Clo. SS3	25 E2	Chelmsford Av. SS2	22 B3	Cobham Rd. SS0	2?
Brookside. SS5	9 F5	Carnarvon Rd. SS2	5 A1	Chelmsford Rd. SS6	6 B1	Cockethurst Clo. SS0	2?
Broomfield. SS7	18 D1	Carnival Gdns. SS9	20 C1	Chelsea Av. SS1	23 F6	Cokefield Av. SS2	2?
Broomfield Av. SS9	16 A5	Caro Rd. SS8	28 D4	Chelsworth Clo. SS1	23 G4	Coker Rd. SS8	2?
Broomfield Av. SS6	6 C3	Carolines Clo. SS2	17 F5	Chelsworth Cres. SS1	23 G4	Colbert Av. SS1	2?
Broomfield Grn. SS8	28 A3	Cartwright Rd. SS7	12 D2	Cheltenham Dri. SS9	20 D3	Colchester Clo. SS2	2?
Broughton Rd. SS7	19 F3	Cashiobury Ter. SS1	5 A5	Cheltenham Dri. SS7	13 G2	Colchester Rd. SS2	?
Browning Av. SS2	5 C1	Cassel Rd. SS8	28 C3	Cheltenham Rd. SS5	9 F2	Coleman St. SS2	?
Bruges Rd. SS8	28 D5	Castle Av. SS7	18 D4	Cheltenham Rd. SS1	23 E4	Colemans Av. SS0	2?
Brunel Rd. SS9	15 F4	Castle Clo. SS6	7 F5	Cherry Av. SS9	16 B5	College Way. SS1	?
Brunel Rd. SS7	12 D2	Castle Clo. SS3	25 G3	Cherry Clo. SS8	27 E7	Collindale Clo. SS8	28
Brunswick Rd. SS1	23 F4	Castle Ct. SS6	7 F5	Cherry Clo. SS5	9 F2	Collingwood. SS7	1?
Brussum Rd. SS8	29 E6	Castle Dri. SS9	20 A5	Cherry Orchard La. SS4	16 C1	Collingwood Way. SS3	2?
Bruton Av. SS0	16 B5	Castle Dri. SS6	7 E4	Cherry Orchard Way. SS2	16 C3	Collins Way. SS9	1?
Bryant Av. SS1	23 F6	Castle La. SS7	19 E4	Cherrybrook. SS1	24 B2	Colne Dri. SS3	2?
Buckingham Rd. SS5	8 D3	Castle Rd. SS7	19 E4	Cherrydown. SS6	7 F3	Colworth Clo. SS7	1?
Buckland. SS3	24 C2	Castle Rd. SS6	7 F5	Cherrymeade. SS7	13 F4	Comet Way. SS9	1?
Buckwins Sq. SS2	5 A1	Castle Ter. SS6	7 F4	Chertsey Clo. SS3	24 D1	Commercial Rd. SS0	?
Budna Rd. SS8	28 A3	Castle View Rd. SS8	28 B1	Chester Av. SS1	23 F6	Common App. SS7	1?
Bull La. SS5	8 C3	Castle Walk. SS8	28 B2	Chesterfield Av. SS7	12 C3	Common La. SS7	1?
Bull La. SS6	7 F4	Castleton Rd. SS2	23 F3	Chesterfield Cres. SS9	15 G5	Commonhall La. SS7	1?
Bullwood App. SS5	8 C4	Catherine Rd. SS7	12 D5	Chestnut Gro. SS7	12 B5	Compton Ct. SS8	2?
Bullwood Rd. SS5	8 D4	Caulfield Rd. SS3	24 C4	Chestnut Gro. SS2	22 D2	Concord Rd. SS8	2?
Bulow Av. SS8	28 B4	Causton Way. SS6	7 F2	Chestnut Walk. SS8	27 E7	Conifers. SS7	1?
Bulwark Rd. SS3	25 E3	Cavendish Gdns. SS2	21 F3	Chestnut Walk. SS5	9 F3	Coniston. SS2	1?
Bulwood Hall La. SS5	8 B4	Caversham Av. SS3	25 E1	Chevening Gdns. SS5	8 D3	Coniston Clo. SS6	7
Bunters Av. SS3	24 C5	Caversham Pk Av. SS6	7 F1	Chichester Clo. SS8	28 B5	Coniston Rd. SS8	28
Burches Mead. SS7	13 F2	Cecil Way. SS5	7 H4	Chichester Rd. SS1	5 B3	Coniston Rd. SS7	2?
Burches Rd. SS7	4 A6	Cedar Clo. SS6	7 H6	Chiltern App. SS8	27 F6	Connaught Gdns. SS3	2? · 2
Burdett Av. SS0	22 A4	Cedar Clo. SS2	22 C2	Chiltern Clo. SS6	7 F3	Connaught Rd. SS6	1?
		Cedar Hall Gdns. SS7	13 F2	Chinchilla Rd. SS1	23 F4	Connaught Walk. SS6	?
		Cedar Mews. SS5	8 D3	Christchurch Rd. SS2	23 E3		
				Church Clo. SS3	24 D5		

Street	Ref	Street	Ref	Street	Ref	Street	Ref
stable Way. SS3	25 F2	Danescroft Clo. SS9	20 C1	Dunster Av. SS0	16 B5	Essex Clo. SS6	7 H6
stitution Hill. SS7	12 C6	Danescroft Dri. SS9	20 B1	Durham Rd. SS5	9 H4	Essex Gdns. SS9	20 C1
stitution Way. SS7	12 C6	Danesfield. SS7	26 C2	Durham Rd. SS2	23 F2	Essex Rd. SS8	28 D3
vent Rd. SS8	28 C4	Danesleigh Gdns. SS9	20 C1	Durham Way. SS6	7 F1	Essex St. SS1	5 B3
kham Ct. SS3	25 E1	Darenth Rd. SS9	19 H4	Durley Clo. SS7	13 E5	Essex Way. SS7	26 D2
mbes Cnr. SS9	15 H6	Dark La. SS7	13 F3	Dyke Cres. SS8	27 D6	Estate Rd. SS7	19 G3
mbes Gro. SS4	11 H6	Darlinghurst Gro. SS9	21 E3	Dynevor Gdns. SS9	19 H5	Estuary Mews. SS3	24 D4
mbewood Dri. SS7	13 E3	Dartmouth Clo. SS6	7 F2			Ethel Rd. SS6	15 E2
pers Way. SS2	17 H5	Datchet Dri. SS3	24 D1	Eagle Way. SS3	25 E2	Etheldor Av. SS5	9 E1
elands. SS4	10 D2	Dawlish Cres. SS6	7 F1	Earleswood. SS7	12 C5	Eton Clo. SS8	28 C3
ford Av. SS6	7 H5	Dawlish Dri. SS9	20 D4	Earls Hall Av. SS2	22 A1	Eton Walk. SS3	24 D1
per Beeches. SS7	13 H2	Daws Heath Rd,		Earls Hall Par. SS2	17 F6	Evelyn Rd. SS5	9 E4
tfold Clo. SS1	23 H3	Daws Heath. SS7	14 A4	East Cres. SS8	28 A3	Everest. SS6	7 F1
asway. SS7	13 H3	Daws Heath Rd,		East St. SS9	20 C5	Eversley Ct. SS7	12 C2
dena Cres. SS6	7 E3	Thundersley. SS7	14 A2	East St. SS4	11 F6	Eversley Rd. SS7	12 B2
nec Av. SS9	15 E4	Deepdale. SS7	13 E3	East St. SS2	22 B2	Ewan Clo. SS9	19 G3
nec Chase. SS9	15 E4	Deepdene Av. SS6	7 E2	Eastbourne Gro. SS0	21 G2	Ewan Way. SS9	19 G3
nhill Av. SS5	9 E2	Deeping. SS1	5 B3	Eastbury Av. SS4	10 D4	Exeter Clo. SS3	25 F2
nwall Gdns. SS4	10 D4	Deepwater Rd. SS9	27 E6	Eastcheap. SS6	7 E2	Exford Av. SS0	21 F1
nwall Rd. SS2	5 C3	Deerhurst. SS7	13 G2	Eastcote Gro. SS2	23 F2	Exmouth Dri. SS6	7 F1
nworthy. SS3	24 C3	Deerhurst Clo. SS7	13 G2	Eastern Av. SS2	22 C1		
ona Rd. SS8	28 D3	Delaware Cres. SS3	24 D3	Eastern Av. SS7	12 B3	Fairburn Clo. SS1	5 D3
sel Rd. SS8	29 E5	Delaware Rd. SS3	24 C3	Eastern Clo. SS2	22 C1	Fairfax Dri. SS0	22 A2
grove Av. SS9	19 H2	Delder Av. SS8	28 D5	Eastern Esp. SS2	28 D6	Fairfield Cres. SS9	16 A4
sington Rd. SS0	22 A5	Delft Rd. SS8	28 B3	Eastern Esp. SS1	23 F6	Fairfield Gdns. SS9	15 H4
swold Av. SS6	7 F3	Delfzul Rd. SS8	28 B3	Eastern Rd. SS6	7 E6	Fairfield Rd. SS9	15 H4
swold Rd. SS0	21 H5	Delgada Rd. SS8	28 D4	Eastfield Rd. SS8	29 E3	Fairland Clo. SS6	7 G2
tesmore Clo. SS8	28 B5	Delview. SS8	28 A3	Eastleigh Rd. SS7	26 E2	Fairlawn Gdns. SS2	17 E5
tesmore Gdns. SS9	19 G4	Dene Clo. SS6	7 F2	Eastview Dri. SS6	7 G1	Fairleigh Dri. SS9	20 C4
ftsmans Sq. SS2	17 G5	Dene Gdns. SS6	7 F2	Eastway. SS8	28 A3	Fairlight Rd. SS7	13 H6
nbrook Av. SS7	13 H5	Denesmere. SS7	12 C5	Eastwood Back La. SS7	14 C5	Fairlop Av. SS8	28 B4
nleigh Dri. SS9	20 C3	Denham Rd. SS8	28 A3	Eastwood Boulevard. SS0	21 E2	Fairmead. SS6	6 D2
nley Av. SS0	21 H4	Denham Vale. SS6	6 C4	Eastwood Lane Sth. SS0	21 F3	Fairmead Av. SS7	14 B5
nley Gdns. SS0	24 C5	Denton App. SS2	16 D6	Eastwood Old Rd. SS9	15 E4	Fairmead Av. SS0	21 G4
nley Rd. SS0	21 H5	Denton Av. SS2	16 D5	Eastwood Pk Clo. SS9	15 H4	Fairview. SS8	27 F6
nston Av. SS2	16 D5	Denton Clo. SS2	16 D5	Eastwood Pk Dri. SS9	15 H4	Fairview Clo. SS7	12 C2
ven Av. SS8	28 A5	Derbydale. SS4	10 D2	Eastwood Rise. SS9	15 E3	Fairview Cres. SS7	12 C1
ven Clo. SS4	11 E3	Derek Gdns. SS2	17 E5	Eastwood Rd. SS9	20 B3	Fairview Dri. SS0	21 G1
ek Rd. SS8	28 D3	Dering Cres. SS9	15 G4	Eastwood Rd. SS6	7 F5	Fairview Gdns. SS9	20 B3
scent Rd. SS8	29 E5	Derventer Av. SS8	28 A2	Eastwood Rd Nth. SS9	20 B2	Fairview Walk. SS7	12 C1
scent Rd. SS9	19 H4	Derwent Av. SS6	7 G4	Eastwoodbury Clo. SS2	17 E4	Fairway Gdns. SS9	15 F6
scent Rd. SS7	12 D6	Devereux Rd. SS1	5 B5	Eastwoodbury Cres. SS2	17 E4	Fairway Gdns Clo. SS9	15 F5
swick Av. SS6	7 E3	Devon Gdns. SS4	10 D3	Eastwoodbury La. SS9	16 B4	Falbro Cres. SS7	18 D2
cketfield Gro. SS9	20 D3	Devon Way. SS8	28 B2	Eaton Rd. SS9	20 A3	Falcon Clo. SS6	6 D3
ft Clo. SS9	20 C1	Dewyk Rd. SS8	28 C3	Eccles Rd. SS8	29 E4	Falcon Clo. SS9	15 H6
ft Clo. SS7	12 B4	Dickens Clo. SS2	22 D2	Edinburgh Av. SS8	20 A3	Falcon Way. SS9	25 E2
ft Rd. SS7	12 B4	Dinant Av. SS8	27 E6	Edith Clo. SS8	27 D7	Fallowfield. SS3	24 C2
mer Rd. SS1	5 D4	Disraeli Rd. SS6	15 E2	Edith Rd. SS8	27 D7	Fane Rd. SS7	6 A5
omwell Rd. SS5	9 F3	Ditton Court Rd. SS0	21 H5	Edith Rd. SS2	22 B2	Faraday Rd. SS9	15 F4
omwell Rd. SS2	22 D1	Dobsons Clo. SS6	7 G6	Edward Clo. SS4	10 C2	Farm Rd. SS8	28 C3
openburg Wk. SS8	28 B3	Doggetts Chase. SS4	11 G2	Eldbert Clo. SS2	23 G2	Farm View. SS6	7 F1
osby Rd. SS0	21 F5	Doggetts Clo. SS4	11 G5	Elder Tree Rd. SS8	28 C4	Farm Way. SS7	13 G2
oss Rd. SS7	13 C5	Dollant Av. SS8	28 B4	Elderstep Av. SS8	29 F5	Farriers Way. SS2	17 G5
ossfell Rd. SS7	13 E2	Dolphins. SS0	16 D6	Elderton Rd. SS0	21 H5	Farringdon, Service Rd.	
ossfield Rd. SS2	23 F2	Doric Av. SS4	11 E3	Eldon Way. SS5	9 E3	SS1	5 B3
ossways. SS7	27 E7	Dorothy Farm Rd. SS6	14 D1	Electric Av. SS0	21 G4	Fastnet. SS9	16 B3
ouch Way. SS3	24 D4	Dorothy Gdns. SS7	13 F4	Elgar Clo. SS7	12 B3	Featherby Way. SS4	17 G2
ouchview Cres. SS5	9 G1	Dorset Gdns. SS4	10 D3	Eliot Mews. SS7	22 D2	Feeches Rd. SS2	16 D5
owborough Rd. SS6	5 A1	Dorset Way. SS8	28 B2	Elizabeth Av. SS6	7 E6	Felstead Clo. SS7	12 D5
own Gdns. SS6	7 E4	Douglas Rd. SS7	19 F3	Elizabeth Clo. SS5	9 E5	Felstead Rd. SS7	12 C5
own Hill. SS6	7 E4	Doulton Way. SS4	10 D2	Elizabeth Rd. SS1	23 F6	Fenwick Way. SS8	28 B2
own Rd. SS5	8 B4	Dove Dri. SS7	26 B1	Elizabeth Way. SS7	13 H4	Fermoy Rd. SS1	24 A3
owstone Av. SS0	21 G6	Dovecote. SS3	25 E2	Ellen Brook Clo. SS9	20 C2	Fern Walk. SS9	28 A4
owstone Clo. SS0	21 H4	Dovedale. SS8	29 E3	Ellesmere Rd. SS9	27 E8	Fern Wood. SS7	19 E2
owstone Rd. SS0	21 G5	Dovercliff Rd. SS8	29 E5	Elm Clo. SS6	7 F3	Fernbrook Av. SS1	23 F4
mberland Av. SS7	12 B5	Dovervelt Rd. SS8	28 C2	Elm Clo. SS3	24 D3	Ferndale Cres. SS8	28 B6
mberland Av. SS2	23 E2	Dovesgate. SS7	12 B4	Elm Dri. SS6	7 F4	Ferndale Rd. SS6	7 G1
mbria Clo. SS8	27 C7	Downer Rd. SS7	12 D5	Elm Gro. SS1	24 A3	Ferndale Rd. SS2	23 E2
nningham Clo. SS3	25 E2	Downer Rd Nth. SS7	12 D3	Elm Rd. SS8	28 C4	Fernlea Rd. SS7	13 E5
rlew Dri. SS7	26 C1	Downes Way. SS7	12 D6	Elm Rd. SS7	18 D4	Fernleigh Dri. SS9	21 E4
rtis Way. SS6	7 G3	Downhall Clo. SS7	7 F2	Elm Rd. SS9	20 C4	Ferry Mead. SS8	28 A3
		Downhall Pk Way. SS6	7 E1	Elm Rd. SS3	24 D3	Ferry Rd. SS7	26 D3
arle Av. SS8	28 B4	Downhall Rd. SS6	7 F3	Elm View Rd. SS7	12 B5	Fifth Av. SS8	27 E6
ines Clo. SS1	24 B2	Downham Rd. SS8	28 B5	Elmer App. SS1	5 B4	Fillebrook Av. SS9	21 E3
ines Way. SS1	24 A2	Drake Clo. SS7	13 H4	Elmer Av. SS1	5 B4	Finchfield. SS6	7 F5
le Rd. SS9	19 H5	Drake Rd. SS0	21 G4	Elmhurst Av. SS7	12 B4	Finchley Rd. SS0	21 H5
almatia Rd. SS1	23 F4	Drakes Way. SS6	7 G2	Elmsleigh Dri. SS9	20 C2	Fir Walk. SS8	27 F6
alwood. SS3	24 C2	Drewsteignton. SS3	24 D2	Elmwood Av. SS5	9 F5	Firfield Rd. SS7	13 H2
alwood Gdns. SS7	19 E1	Droitwich Av. SS2	23 F3	Elounda Ct. SS7	12 C4	First Av. SS8	27 D7
alys Rd. SS4	11 E6	Dryden Av. SS2	5 C1	Elsinor Av. SS8	28 A2	First Av. SS0	21 F5
anbury Clo. SS9	20 D1	Dubarry Clo. SS7	13 F4	Ely Rd. SS2	5 D1	Fitzwarren. SS3	24 D1
anbury Rd. SS6	6 D3	Dulverton Av. SS0	21 E1	Ely Way. SS6	7 E2	Five Oaks. SS7	13 H5
andies Chase. SS9	15 G4	Dulverton Clo. SS0	16 B6	Endway. SS9	19 E3	Flamborough Clo. SS9	15 F4
andies Clo. SS9	15 G4	Dundee Av. SS9	20 A3	Englefield Clo. SS5	9 G5	Flamborough Wk. SS9	15 F4
ane St. SS3	25 F5	Dundee Clo. SS9	20 A3	Ennismore Gdns. SS2	22 C1	Fleet Rd. SS7	26 D1
anes Av. SS3	25 E5	Dundonald Dri. SS9	21 E4	Epping Clo. SS9	15 G4	Fleetwood Av. SS0	21 G4
		Dungannon Chase. SS1	24 B4	Esplanade Gdns. SS0	21 F5	Flemming Av. SS9	20 B2
		Dungannon Dri. SS1	24 B5	Essex Clo. SS8	28 A5	Flemming Cres. SS9	20 B2

Name	Ref	Name	Ref	Name	Ref	Name	Ref
Flemings Farm Rd. SS9	15 G3	Goldfinch La. SS7	13 F1	Hadleigh Rd. SS0	22 A5	Heather Dri. SS7	1
Fletchers Square. SS2	17 G5	Goldhanger Clo. SS6	6 D3	Hainault Av. SS4	10 D4	Heathfield. SS6	
Florence Clo. SS7	18 D3	Goldmer Clo. SS3	24 C3	Hainault Av. SS0	21 H3	Heathfield. SS7	1
Florence Gdns. SS7	18 D3	Golf Ride. SS7	12 D6	Hainault Clo. SS7	19 E1	Hedge La. SS7	1
Florence Rd. SS8	28 D4	Goodwood Clo. SS7	13 G2	Hall Cres. SS7	18 D2	Hedgehope Av. SS6	
Foksville Rd. SS8	28 C4	Goor Av. SS8	29 E4	Hall Farm Clo. SS7	26 D2	Hedingham Pl. SS4	1
Folly Chase. SS5	8 C3	Gordon Pl. SS1	5 A4	Hall Farm Rd. SS7	26 D1	Heeswyk Rd. SS8	2
Folly La. SS5	8 C3	Gordon Rd. SS9	20 A3	Hall Park Av. SS0	21 F5	Heideburg Rd. SS8	2
Forest Av. SS1	5 C5	Gordon Rd. SS1	5 A3	Hall Park Way. SS0	21 F5	Heilsburg Rd. SS8	2
Forest View Dri. SS9	19 G2	Gosfield Clo. SS6	6 C3	Hall Rd. SS4	9 F6	Helden Av. SS8	2
Forfar Clo. SS9	20 A3	Gowan Brae. SS7	12 B4	Hallett Rd. SS8	29 E4	Helena Clo. SS5	
Fortescue Chase. SS1	23 H3	Gowan Clo. SS7	12 B4	Hambro Av. SS6	7 F2	Helena Rd. SS6	
Fossetts Way. SS2	23 E1	Gowan Ct. SS7	12 B4	Hambro Clo. SS6	7 G2	Hellendoorn Rd. SS8	2
Fostal Clo. SS9	20 D2	Goya Rise. SS3	25 F2	Hambro Gdns. SS9	19 H5	Henley Cres. SS0	2
Foster Rd. SS8	28 D3	Grafton Rd. SS8	28 C5	Hambro Hill. SS6	7 G2	Henry Dri. SS9	19
Fountain La. SS5	8 B4	Graham Clo. SS5	9 F2	Hambro Parade. SS6	7 F1	Henson Av. SS8	2
Fourth Walk. SS8	27 E6	Grainger Clo. SS2	5 B1	Hamilton Clo. SS9	19 G3	Herbert Gro. SS1	
Fowler Clo. SS1	5 D3	Grainger Rd. SS2	5 B2	Hamilton Gdns. SS5	9 E2	Herbert Rd. SS8	2
Fox Clo. SS7	13 E3	Grand Dri. SS9	20 D5	Hamilton Mews. SS6	7 H3	Herbert Rd. SS3	2
Fox Hall La. SS2	23 G1	Grand Par. SS9	20 D5	Hamlet Court Rd. SS0	22 A4	Heritage Pl. SS4	1
Foxfield Clo. SS5	9 G3	Grandview Rd. SS7	13 E2	Hamlet Ct Mews. SS0	22 A4	Hermes Way. SS3	2
Foxmeadows. SS7	13 E3	Grange Av. SS9	19 G1	Hamlet Rd. SS1	5 A4	Hermitage Av. SS7	13
Foxwood Pl. SS9	20 B3	Grange Clo. SS9	20 C2	Hampstead Gdns. SS5	10 A1	Hermitage Clo. SS7	13
Francis Walk. SS6	7 F4	Grange Gdns. SS6	6 D3	Hampton Clo. SS2	17 E6	Hermitage Rd. SS0	22
Fraser Clo. SS3	25 E2	Grange Gdns. SS1	5 C4	Hampton Ct. SS5	8 D3	Hernen Rd. SS8	28
Freemantle. SS3	24 D5	Grange Park Dri. SS9	21 E3	Hampton Gdns. SS2	17 E6	Heron Gdns. SS6	6
Friars St. SS3	25 F4	Grange Rd. SS9	20 C4	Hamstel Rd. SS2	23 F1	Herongate. SS7	12
Frobisher Way. SS3	24 D2	Grange Rd. SS7	13 E1	Handel Rd. SS8	28 D5	Herongate. SS3	25
Fulford Dri. SS9	16 A4	Grangeway. SS7	13 F2	Hanley Clo. SS7	12 A2	Herschell Rd. SS9	20
Fulton Rd. SS7	12 D2	Grangewood. SS7	12 C4	Hannah Clo. SS8	28 B2	Hertford Rd. SS8	28
Furtherwick Rd. SS8	28 C4	Granville Clo. SS7	12 D5	Hannett Rd. SS8	29 F4	Hetzand Dri. SS8	29
Fyfield Path. SS6	6 D3	Grasmead Av. SS9	21 E3	Hanningfield Clo. SS6	6 C3	Hever Clo. SS5	8
		Grasmere Rd. SS8	27 E8	Hanover Mews. SS5	8 D3	Heycroft Rd. SS9	16
Gafzelle Dri. SS8	29 E5	Grasmere Rd. SS7	13 E3	Harberts Way. SS6	7 F1	Heycroft Rd. SS5	9
Gains Clo. SS8	28 D4	Gravel Rd. SS9	15 E3	Harcourt Av. SS2	5 A1	Heygate Av. SS1	5
Gainsborough Av. SS8	29 E5	Graysons Clo. SS6	7 G4	Hardwick Clo. SS6	7 G6	Hickling Clo. SS9	15
Gainsborough Dri. SS0	22 A1	Great Burches Rd. SS7	13 F2	Hardys Way. SS8	28 A1	High Beeches. SS7	12
Galleydene. SS7	18 D3	Great Eastern Av. SS2	5 B2	Haresland Clo. SS7	14 C5	High Cliff Dri. SS9	20
Galton Rd. SS0	21 F5	Great Eastern Rd. SS5	9 E4	Harewood Av. SS4	10 D3	High Mead. SS5	9
Garon Park. SS20	23 F1	Great Hays. SS9	15 F5	Harley St. SS9	20 A4	High Mead. SS6	7
Gatscombe Clo. SS5	8 D3	Great Wheatley Rd. SS6	6 D5	Haron Clo. SS8	28 C4	High Rd. SS5	8
Gay Bowyers. SS5	8 C3	Green Av. SS8	27 E7	Harper Clo. SS6	7 F3	High Rd. SS6	7
Gay Leighs. SS5	7 F3	Green Dyke. SS8	27 F6	Harridge Clo. SS9	20 D2	High Rd,	
Gayton Rd. SS2	5 B1	Green La. SS8	28 A5	Harridge Rd. SS9	20 D2	Sth Benfleet. SS7	26
Geesh Rd. SS8	28 D3	Green La. SS9	15 G3	*Harrier Clo,		High Rd,	
Genesta Rd. SS0	21 G5	Green Rd. SS7	26 D2	Falcon Way. SS3	25 E2	Thundersley. SS7	12
Genk Clo. SS8	28 B2	Green Way. SS4	11 F5	Harrogate Dri. SS5	9 G2	High St, Benfleet. SS7	26
Gennep Rd. SS8	28 C3	Greenacre Mews. SS9	20 D3	Harrogate Rd. SS5	9 F2	High St. SS8	28
Gennep Rd Sth. SS8	28 C3	Greenacres. SS7	19 F2	Harrow Clo. SS5	9 G4	High St, Hadleigh. SS7	18
George St. SS3	25 F4	Greenbanks. SS9	21 E3	Harrow Gdns. SS5	9 G4	High St. SS9	20
Geylen Rd. SS8	29 E4	Greenlands. SS4	11 E5	Harrow Rd. SS8	28 C3	High St. SS3	25
Gifford Rd. SS7	12 C4	Greenleas. SS7	13 G3	Hart Clo. SS7	13 F3	High St. SS1	5
Gifhorn Rd. SS8	29 E4	Greenoaks. SS7	13 E5	Hart Rd. SS7	13 F2	High St. SS6	7
Gilbert Clo. SS6	7 H5	Greensward La. SS5	9 G2	Hartford Clo. SS6	6 D2	Highams Rd. SS5	9
Gills Av. SS8	28 D3	Greenways. SS8	28 A3	Hartington Pl. SS1	5 D5	Highbank Clo. SS9	16
Gipson Park Clo. SS9	15 F4	Greenways. SS4	11 G6	Hartington Rd. SS1	5 D5	Highcliff Rd. SS7	26
Gladstone Gdns. SS6	7 E6	Greenways. SS7	26 C1	Hartland Clo. SS9	15 G4	Highcliffe Cres. SS4	10
Gladstone Rd. SS5	9 E4	Greenways. SS1	23 G5	Harvard Ct. SS6	6 D2	Highfield Av. SS7	13
Glasseys La. SS6	7 E6	Greenwood Av. SS7	26 D2	Harvest Rd. SS8	28 C3	Highfield Clo. SS0	22
Glastonbury Chase. SS0	16 B5	Gregory Clo. SS5	9 F5	Hassell Rd. SS8	29 E4	Highfield Cres. SS6	7
Glebe Clo. SS6	7 E3	Greyhound Way. SS2	5 C2	Hastings Rd. SS1	5 D4	Highfield Cres. SS0	22
Glebe Clo. SS1	23 G5	Griffin Av. SS8	28 C3	Hatfield Rd. SS6	6 D3	Highfield Dri. SS0	21
Glebe Dri. SS6	7 E3	Grosvenor Mews. SS0	21 G6	Hatley Gdns. SS7	12 B4	Highfield Gdns. SS0	22
Glebe Way. SS7	19 F3	Grosvenor Rd. SS7	26 E2	Haven Clo. SS8	27 D8	Highfield Gro. SS0	22
Glebelands. SS7	12 A2	Grosvenor Rd. SS0	21 G6	Haven Rd. SS8	27 D8	Highfield Way. SS0	21
Glen Rd. SS9	21 E5	Grove Clo. SS6	7 H4	Havestock Clo. SS6	6 C3	Highlands Boulevard. SS9	19 C
Glen Rd. SS7	13 E4	Grove Ct. SS6	14 D1	Hawkesbury Clo. SS8	27 F8	Highview Rd. SS7	13
Glenbervie Dri. SS9	21 E3	Grove Hill. SS6	15 E4	Hawkesbury Rd. SS8	27 F8	Highwood Clo. SS9	20
Glendale Gdns. SS9	20 B4	Grove Rd. SS8	28 D3	Hawkridge. SS3	24 C2	Hilary Clo. SS4	11
Gleneagles. SS7	12 B3	Grove Rd. SS6	7 H5	Hawkwell Chase. SS5	9 F4	Hilary Cres. SS6	7
Gleneagles Rd. SS9	15 F6	Grove Rd. SS7	12 D6	Hawkwell Park Dri. SS5	9 F4	Hilbery Rd. SS8	28
Glenhurst Rd. SS2	22 C2	Grove Walk. SS3	25 E4	Hawkwell Rd. SS5	9 F3	Hildaville Dri. SS0	21
Glenmere Pk Av. SS9	13 G5	Grovewood Av. SS9	15 E4	Hawthorn Clo. SS9	9 G4	Hill Clo. SS7	12
Glenmore St. SS2	23 F3	Grovewood Clo. SS9	15 E4	Hawthorn Rd. SS8	28 C4	Hill La. SS5	9
Glenriddings. SS7	12 C4	Guildford Rd. SS2	5 B2	Hawthorn Way. SS6	7 H6	Hill Rd. SS7	12
Glenwood. SS8	28 A3	Gunfleet. SS3	24 C3	Hawthorne Gdns. SS7	8 B3	Hill Rd. SS2	23
Glenwood Av. SS9	15 E3	Gunners Rd. SS3	25 F4	Hawthorns. SS9	20 C1	Hill View Rd. SS6	7
Glenwood Av. SS5	9 G4	Gusted Hall La. SS5	9 E6	Hawthorns. SS7	12 C5	Hillborough Rd. SS0	21
Glenwood Av. SS0	22 A2	Gwendalen Av. SS8	28 D4	Hawtree Clo. SS1	23 E5	Hillcrest Rd. SS5	9
Gleton Rd. SS8	29 E4			Hayes Barton. SS1	24 C2	Hillcrest Rd. SS1	5
Gloucester Av. SS6	14 D2	Haarle Rd. SS8	29 E6	Hayes La. SS8	28 A5	Hillside Av. SS5	9
Gloucester Ter. SS1	23 H6	Haarlem Rd. SS8	27 D6	Hazel Clo. SS7	19 F3	Hillside Cres. SS9	21
Glyders. SS7	26 E2	Haase Clo. SS8	28 B2	Hazel Clo. SS9	20 A3	Hillside Rd. SS6	8
Glynde Way. SS2	23 G3	Hackamore. SS7	13 G3	Hazeldene. SS6	7 F2	Hillside Rd,	
Goirle Av. SS8	28 C3	Hacks Dri. SS7	13 H1	Hazelwood. SS8	28 D4	Leigh-on-Sea. SS9	20 C
Golden Cross Par. SS4	11 E4	Haddon Clo. SS6	6 C3	Hazelwood. SS7	12 B1	Hillside Rd, Rayleigh. SS9	15 F
Golden Cross Rd. SS4	11 E2	Hadleigh Park Av. SS7	13 H5	Hazelwood Gro. SS9	15 H5	Hillside Rd. SS7	26 C
Golden Manor Dri. SS7	13 F3	Hadleigh Rd. SS9	20 A4	Hazlemere Rd. SS7	12 C3	Hilltop Av. SS7	13

Street	Ref
p Clo. SS6	7 E5
ay. SS0	21 F5
n Rd. SS8	28 B2
rsum Way. SS8	28 B3
les Rd. SS8	28 D3
uar St. SS3	25 F4
eythick La. SS0	22 A1
ley Rise. SS5	9 E4
ley Rd. SS6	7 F4
arth Dri. SS3	25 F3
arth Way. SS4	10 D4
ek Rd. SS8	29 E4
and Av. SS8	27 D6
and Rd. SS0	22 A5
y Ct. SS5	9 E4
y Walk. SS8	28 A4
ytree Gdns. SS6	7 E6
sdale Clo. SS0	21 G2
swood. SS8	29 E3
worthy. SS3	24 D3
Farm Way. SS4	10 D4
on Rd. SS8	29 F4
on Rd. SS6	14 D1
ynge. SS7	12 C5
oak La. SS5	9 E5
rood Dri. SS0	21 F3
efields Av. SS7	12 B3
estead Gdns. SS7	18 D3
estead Rd. SS7	19 E3
estead Way. SS7	18 D3
ton Rd. SS1	5 D4
e Rd. SS8	29 E5
e Rd. SS7	26 C1
ace Rd. SS1	5 C4
beams. SS7	12 B1
by Av. SS2	16 D5
by Clo. SS2	17 E5
sland Rd. SS8	29 F4
pital Rd. SS3	25 F5
ard Pl. SS8	28 C5
ards Chase. SS2	22 B2
son Cres. SS9	15 G5
son Rd. SS9	15 G5
son Way. SS8	28 B2
bridge Rd. SS6	7 F1
ber Clo. SS6	7 E5
ngton Rd. SS1	23 F4
e Wood La. SS4	11 F1
eway. SS7	13 F3
combe Av. SS1	23 E4
combe Rd. SS2	23 E3
erial Av. SS0	21 G4
USTRIAL ESTATES:	
ook Rd Ind Est. SS6	14 A2
arfleets Ind Est. SS7	27 C7
urence Ind Est. SS9	16 C4
anor Trading Est. SS7	12 D2
rdeys Ind Est. SS4	17 G2
wreth Ind Est. SS6	4 D1
yleigh Weir Ind Est. SS7	14 A3
vaines Ind Est. SS4	11 E5
rness Av. SS0	22 A2
well La. SS5	9 G6
gton Clo. SS9	20 C1
Rd. SS7	12 A3
Walk. SS8	28 A3
kdaw Clo. SS3	25 E2
ette Av. SS8	27 E8
vis Rd. SS8	28 B2
vis Rd. SS7	12 D4
on Clo. SS8	28 C3
a Clo. SS3	24 D4
mond Rd. SS8	28 C5
n St. SS3	25 F5
nson Clo. SS4	11 E3
nstone Rd. SS1	24 A4
es Clo. SS2	22 A1
es Corner. SS9	15 G4
mans La. SS1	12 A6
rneymans Way. SS2	17 G5
ilee Clo. SS5	9 E4
ilee Rd. SS6	7 G4
ers Clo. SS8	28 D5
ers Rd. SS8	28 D5
Juniper Rd. SS9	21 E1
Kale Rd. SS7	12 D5
Kamerwyk Av. SS8	28 D3
Karen Clo. SS7	26 D2
Katherine Clo. SS6	14 D1
Kathleen Dri. SS9	20 D3
Keats Walk. SS6	14 D1
Keegan Pl. SS8	28 D4
Keer Av. SS8	29 E5
Keighley Mews. SS3	24 D1
Keith Way. SS2	17 E5
Kellington Rd. SS8	28 C2
Kelvedon Clo. SS6	6 D3
Kelvin Rd. SS7	12 D1
Kembles. SS6	7 G2
Kempton Clo. SS7	13 H1
Ken Holme. SS9	20 C1
Kendal Clo. SS6	7 G4
Kendal Way. SS9	15 H3
Kenilworth Gdns. SS6	7 E3
Kenilworth Gdns. SS0	21 E2
Kenmore Clo. SS8	29 F5
Kennedy Clo. SS6	14 D2
Kenneth Rd. SS8	28 D2
Kenneth Rd. SS7	13 E3
Kennington Av. SS7	12 B3
Kensington Rd. SS1	23 F4
Kensington Way. SS5	8 D3
Kent Av. SS8	28 C2
Kent Av. SS9	20 D3
Kent Elms Clo. SS9	16 A5
Kent Green Clo. SS5	9 F4
Kent View Av. SS9	21 E5
Kent Way. SS6	14 D2
Kents Hills Rd. SS7	12 C5
Kents Hills Rd Nth. SS7	12 D3
Kenway. SS2	22 C2
Kestrel Gro. SS6	6 D3
Keswick Clo. SS6	7 G4
Keswick Rd. SS7	12 D2
Keyes Clo. SS3	25 E2
Keysland. SS7	13 G2
Kiln Rd. SS7	13 E4
Kilnwood Av. SS5	9 E4
Kilworth Av. SS1	5 D4
Kimberley Rd. SS7	12 B5
King Georges Clo. SS6	7 F5
King Henrys Dri. SS4	17 F3
Kingfisher Clo. SS3	25 E2
Kingfisher Cres. SS6	6 D4
Kingfisher Dri. SS7	26 C1
Kings Clo. SS8	27 C7
Kings Clo. SS6	7 G4
Kings Farm. SS6	7 G1
Kings Park. SS7	13 E3
Kings Rd. SS8	27 C7
Kings Rd. SS0	21 E4
Kings Rd. SS6	7 G5
Kings Rd. SS7	26 E1
Kingsdown Walk. SS8	28 A2
Kingshawes. SS7	13 G3
Kingsley Cres. SS7	13 H1
Kingsley La. SS7	13 G1
Kingsmere. SS7	13 H4
Kingsteignton. SS3	24 C2
Kingston Av. SS3	25 E1
Kingston Way. SS7	13 E3
Kingsway. SS0	21 F3
Kingsway Mews. SS0	21 F3
Kingswood Chase. SS9	20 C2
Kingswood Cres. SS6	6 D6
Kipling Mews. SS2	22 D2
Kitkatts Farm Rd. SS8	28 B4
Kitkatts Rd. SS8	28 B5
Klondyke Av. SS8	6 D4
Knightswick Rd. SS8	28 C4
Knivet Clo. SS6	7 G6
Knollcroft. SS3	24 D5
Kolburg Rd. SS8	28 D5
Kollum Rd. SS8	29 F4
Koln Clo. SS8	27 C8
Komberg Cres. SS8	28 D2
Konny Brook. SS7	13 F4
Korndyk Av. SS8	28 C4
Kursaal Way. SS1	23 E5
Laars Av.SS8	28 D3
Laburnum Clo. SS5	8 C3
Laburnum Gro. SS8	27 D8
Laburnum Gro. SS5	8 C3
Labworth La. SS8	28 D5
Labworth Rd. SS8	28 C5
Ladram Clo. SS1	24 B2
Ladram Rd. SS1	24 B2
Ladram Way. SS1	24 B2
Lake Dri. SS7	13 E4
Lakeside. SS6	7 F2
Lakeside Path. SS8	28 B3
Lakeview. SS8	28 A3
Lambeth Mews. SS5	8 D3
Lambeth Rd. SS9	15 G5
Lambeth Rd. SS7	12 B3
Lambourn Clo. SS3	24 D1
Lancaster Cres. SS1	5 C3
Lancaster Gdns. SS6	14 D2
Lancaster Gdns. SS1	5 C3
Lancaster Rd. SS6	14 D2
Landsburg Rd. SS8	29 E3
Langdon Rd. SS6	7 E3
Langford Cres. SS7	13 E2
Langham Dri. SS6	6 C3
Langley Clo. SS9	15 E3
Langport Dri. SS0	21 F1
Lansdown Av. SS7	14 C5
Lansdown Dri. SS6	7 E4
Lansdowne Av. SS9	21 E4
Lap Water Clo. SS9	20 B3
Lappmark Rd. SS8	29 E4
Larchwood Clo. SS9	15 E4
Larkfield Clo. SS4	11 E4
Larup Av. SS8	28 C4
Larup Gdns. SS8	28 C3
Lascelles Gdns. SS4	10 D3
Latchington Clo. SS6	6 D3
Laurel Clo. SS9	20 C5
Laurence Ind Est. SS9	16 C4
Lavender Gro. SS0	21 H2
Lavender Mews. SS0	21 H2
Lawn Av. SS2	22 D2
Lea Rd. SS7	12 C4
Leamington Rd. SS5	10 A1
Leamington Rd. SS1	23 E4
Leas Clo. SS0	21 F5
Leas Gdns. SS0	21 F5
Leaside. SS7	12 B3
Leasway. SS6	7 E4
Leather La. SS1	5 B3
Lede Rd. SS8	28 B3
Leecon Way. SS4	11 E5
Leicester Av. SS4	17 F3
Leige Av. SS8	28 B2
Leigh Beck La. SS8	29 F5
Leigh Beck Rd. SS8	29 F5
Leigh Cliff Rd. SS9	20 D5
Leigh Gdns. SS9	20 A4
Leigh Hall Rd. SS9	20 D4
Leigh Heights. SS7	19 F3
Leigh Hill. SS9	20 C5
Leigh Hill Clo. SS9	20 C5
Leigh Park Clo. SS9	20 B4
Leigh Park Rd. SS9	20 C5
Leigh Rd. SS8	28 C6
Leigh Rd. SS9	20 D4
Leigh View Dri. SS9	20 D1
Leigham Ct Dri. SS9	20 D4
Leighcroft Gdns. SS9	20 C1
Leighfields. SS7	13 G3
Leighfields Av. SS9	15 G4
Leighfields Rd. SS9	15 F4
Leighton Av. SS9	20 D4
Leighton Rd. SS7	12 B1
Leighville Gro. SS9	20 C4
Leigwood Av. SS9	15 G6
Leitrim Av. SS3	24 C5
Lekoe Rd. SS8	28 A2
Leonard Dri. SS6	6 C3
Leonard Rd. SS0	22 A5
Leslie Clo. SS9	15 G5
Leslie Dri. SS9	15 F5
Leslie Gdns. SS9	7 H6
Leslie Rd. SS6	7 H6
Lesney Gdns. SS4	11 E5
Letzen Rd. SS8	28 B3
Lever La. SS4	17 F1
Lewes Rd. SS2	23 E1
Lewes Way. SS7	13 G2
Leyd Rd. SS8	28 B4
Lifstan Way. SS1	23 G6
Lilac Av. SS8	28 C3
Lilian Pl. SS6	14 D2
Lillyville Walk. SS6	14 D2
Limburg Rd. SS8	27 D6
Lime Av. SS9	20 B3
Lime Ct. SS5	9 E3
Lime Rd. SS7	13 E5
Limetree Av. SS7	12 B5
Limetree Rd. SS8	29 E4
Lincoln Chase. SS2	23 F2
Lincoln Rd. SS4	10 C3
Lincoln Way. SS8	28 A3
Lincoln Way. SS6	7 E1
Linde Rd. SS8	28 C4
Linden Clo. SS6	7 H5
Linden Clo. SS7	12 C3
Linden Leas. SS7	12 C3
Linden Rd. SS7	12 C3
Linden Way. SS8	28 A4
Lindisfarne Av. SS9	21 E3
Lindsey Ct. SS6	6 C3
Lingfield Dri. SS4	11 G6
Link Rd. SS8	28 A3
Link Rd. SS6	7 F3
Links Way. SS7	19 F3
Linksway. SS9	20 A1
Linne Rd. SS8	28 C3
Linnet Clo. SS3	25 E2
Linnet Dri. SS7	26 C1
Linroping Av. SS8	29 F4
Linton Rd. SS3	24 D5
Lionel Rd. SS8	28 B4
Little Fretches. SS9	20 C1
Little Gypps Clo. SS8	28 A4
Little Gypps Rd. SS8	28 A4
Little Hays. SS9	15 E5
Little Stambridge Hall La. SS4	11 H6
Little Thorpe. SS1	24 A2
Little Wheatley Chase. SS6	6 C3
Littons Av. SS9	20 C5
Lloydwise Clo. SS2	23 F1
Locks Hill. SS4	17 F1
Locksley Clo. SS2	23 G2
Lodge Clo. SS6	7 G5
Lodge Clo. SS7	13 F4
Lodge Farm Clo. SS9	15 G6
Lodgelands Clo. SS6	14 C1
Lodwick. SS3	24 C5
London Hill. SS6	7 F4
London Rd, Hadleigh. SS7	19 G3
London Rd. SS9	20 A3
London Rd. SS6	6 B2
London Rd. SS1	5 A3
London Rd, Thundersley. SS7	12 A3
Long Rd. SS8	28 A4
Longsand. SS3	24 C3
Lonsdale Rd. SS2	23 F2
Lord Roberts Av. SS9	21 E4
Lornes Clo. SS2	23 F1
Loten Rd. SS7	26 B1
Lottem Rd. SS8	28 D6
Louis Dri. SS6	6 C3
Louis Dri East. SS6	6 D3
Louis Dri West. SS6	6 C3
Louisa Av. SS7	12 B3
Louise Rd. SS6	7 G4
Love La. SS6	7 E4
Lovelace Av. SS1	23 F4
Lovelace Gdns. SS2	23 F3
Lovell Rise. SS9	16 B4
Lovens Clo. SS8	28 D6
Low Rd. SS3	25 E6
Lower Church Rd. SS7	12 B3
Lower Lambricks. SS6	7 G2
Lubbards Clo. SS6	7 F1
Lucy Rd. SS1	5 C5
Luker Rd. SS1	5 B4
Lundy Clo. SS3	16 C3
Lydford Rd. SS0	22 A5
Lylt Rd. SS8	28 B4
Lyme Rd. SS2	23 E3
Lymington Av. SS9	20 C3
Lympstone Clo. SS9	16 B5

Name	Ref.
Lyndale Av. SS2	22 D2
Lyndene. SS7	12 B3
Lynn View Clo. SS7	12 B4
Lynton Rd. SS1	23 H6
Lynton Rd,. SS7	13 H6
Lynwood Grn. SS6	14 D3
McDivitt Walk. SS9	16 B4
Macdonald Av. SS4	22 A2
Macintyres Walk. SS4	10 D2
Macmurdo Clo. SS9	15 F4
Macmurdo Rd. SS9	15 F4
Madeira Av. SS9	20 D3
Magazine Rd. SS3	25 E5
Magnolia Rd. SS5	9 G3
Magnolia Way. SS4	17 H2
Main Rd, Hawkwell. SS5	9 E4
Main Rd, Hockley. SS5	8 D4
Maine Cres. SS6	6 D2
Maitland Pl. SS3	25 E1
Maldon Rd. SS2	5 B2
Mallards. SS3	25 E2
Malms Mead. SS3	24 C2
Malting Villas. SS4	11 F6
Malvern Av. SS8	27 D8
Malvern Clo. SS6	7 F3
Malvern Rd. SS5	9 F1
Malwood Dri. SS7	12 A3
Malwood Rd. SS7	12 A4
Malyon Court Clo. SS7	13 G5
Manchester Dri. SS9	20 C3
Mandeville Way. SS7	12 B1
Manilla Rd. SS1	23 E5
Mannering Gdns. SS0	21 F2
Manners Way. SS2	17 F6
Manns Way. SS6	7 F1
Manor Clo. SS6	7 F6
Manor Rd. SS5	8 C3
Manor Rd. SS7	12 C3
Manor Rd. SS0	21 H6
Manor Trading Est. SS7	12 D2
Mansel Clo. SS9	15 G5
Mansted Gdns. SS4	11 E3
Maple Av. SS9	20 D5
Maple Sq. SS2	5 C1
Maple Way. SS8	28 A4
Mapleleaf Clo. SS5	10 A1
Maplesfield. SS7	18 D2
Maplin Clo. SS7	12 C2
Maplin Mews. SS3	25 E4
Maplin Way. SS1	24 B3
Maplin Way Nth. SS1	24 C3
Marcos Rd. SS8	28 D5
Marcus Av. SS1	24 B5
Marcus Chase. SS1	24 B4
Marcus Gdns. SS1	24 B4
Margraten Av. SS8	29 E5
Marguerite Dri. SS9	20 D4
Marina Av. SS6	7 F3
Marina Clo. SS2	17 F6
Marine App. SS8	28 C5
Marine Av. SS8	29 E5
Marine Av. SS9	20 B4
Marine Av. SS0	22 B5
Marine Clo. SS9	19 G5
Marine Par. SS8	29 F5
Marine Par. SS9	19 G5
Marine Par. SS1	5 C5
Market Pl. SS1	5 B5
Market Sq. SS4	11 F6
Marks Ct. SS1	5 D5
Marlborough Clo. SS7	12 C2
Marlborough Rd. SS3	23 F4
Marlborough Wk. SS5	8 D3
Marlin Clo. SS7	14 B4
Marlow Gdns. SS2	17 E6
Marmaduke Av. SS6	6 D2
Marsh Rd. SS3	25 E6
Marshall Clo. SS9	19 G3
Marshalls. SS1	11 E5
Marshalls Clo. SS6	7 H4
Martin Walk. SS5	9 F5
Martins Mews. SS7	12 C4
Martingale. SS7	13 H3
Martock Av. SS0	16 B5
Martyns Gro. SS0	21 F3
Marylands Av. SS5	9 E2
Matlock Rd. SS8	28 A4
Maurice Rd. SS8	28 D5
May Av. SS8	28 D4
Maya Clo. SS3	24 D4
Mayfield Av. SS2	22 A1
Mayflower Clo. SS9	16 B4
Mayflower Ct. SS8	28 D6
Mayflowers. SS7	12 B1
Mayland Av. SS8	28 A5
Maytree Walk. SS7	12 C3
Mead Way. SS6	7 H5
Meadow Clo. SS7	13 G2
Meadow Dri. SS1	23 G5
Meadow Rd. SS7	19 F3
Meadow Side. SS6	7 F5
Meadow View. SS6	27 E7
Meadow View Wk. SS8	27 E7
Meadow Way. SS5	9 E3
Meadway. SS8	28 D6
Meadway. SS7	12 C2
Meakins Clo. SS9	16 A4
Medway Cres. SS9	19 H4
Meesons Mead. SS4	11 E5
Meggison Way. SS7	12 C6
Melcombe Rd. SS7	12 C6
Mendip Clo. SS6	7 G3
Mendip Cres. SS0	16 A5
Mendip Rd. SS0	21 E1
Meppel Av. SS8	28 B2
Merilies Clo. SS0	21 F2
Merilies Gdns. SS0	21 F2
Merrivale. SS7	26 C2
Merryfield. SS9	20 D2
Merryfield App. SS9	20 D2
Merryfields Av. SS5	9 E2
Merton Rd. SS7	12 B5
Mess Rd, SS3	25 E6
Meteor Rd. SS0	21 H5
Metz Av. SS8	28 B3
Mey Walk. SS5	8 D3
Meyel Av. SS8	28 C3
Meynell Av. SS8	28 C5
Middle Mead. SS4	11 F6
Middleburg Rd. SS8	27 E6
Middlesex Av. SS9	21 E3
Midhurst Av. SS0	21 H1
Midsummer Mdw. SS3	24 D2
Milbanke Clo. SS8	25 E2
Mill Field Clo. SS6	7 G4
Mill Hill. SS7	26 E2
Mill La. SS4	11 H6
Millhead Way. SS4	17 H2
Millview Meadow. SS4	17 G1
Milton Av. SS0	22 A5
Milton Clo. SS2	5 B2
Milton Clo. SS6	14 D1
Milton Pl. SS1	5 A5
Milton Rd. SS0	22 A5
Milton St. SS2	5 B2
Miltsin Av. SS8	28 D3
Minster Clo. SS6	14 D2
Minton Heights. SS6	10 D2
Miramar Av. SS8	27 E7
Mitchells Av. SS8	28 D3
Moat End. SS1	24 B2
Moat Rise. SS6	7 F6
Montague Av. SS9	20 A3
Montague Pl. SS8	27 E8
Montgomery Ct. SS3	25 E1
Moons Clo. SS4	10 D1
Moor Park Clo. SS9	15 F6
Moor Park Gdns. SS9	15 F6
Moorcroft. SS4	10 D2
Moorcroft Av. SS7	14 B5
Moreland Av. SS7	12 C2
Moreland Clo. SS7	12 C2
Mornington Av. SS4	11 G6
Mornington Cres. SS8	28 D3
Mornington Cres. SS7	19 F3
Mornington Rd. SS8	28 C3
Mortimer Rd. SS6	7 G1
Moseley St. SS2	23 F3
Mount Av. SS0	21 E4
Mount Av. SS5	9 E3
Mount Av. SS6	7 F4
Mount Bovers La. SS5	9 E6
Mount Clo. SS6	7 E4
Mount Cres. SS5	9 E3
Mount Cres. SS7	13 E4
Mount Rd. SS7	13 E4
Mountain Ash Clo. SS9	15 E5
Mountain Ash Av. SS9	15 E5
Mountbatten Dri. SS3	25 E1
Mountdale Gdns. SS3	20 D1
Mountnessing. SS7	18 D3
Muir Way. SS7	12 B2
Mulberry Rd. SS8	27 C7
Munsterburg Rd. SS8	29 E3
Murrels La. SS5	6 A2
Musket Gro. SS9	15 E4
Namur Rd. SS8	28 D3
Nansen Av. SS8	11 E2
Napier Av. SS1	5 B4
Napier Gdns. SS7	13 H3
Napier Rd. SS6	7 H3
Navestock Gdns. SS1	23 H4
Neil Armstrong Way. SS9	16 B4
Nelson Clo. SS6	7 H3
Nelson Dri. SS9	21 E4
Nelson Gdns. SS6	7 H3
Nelson Mews. SS1	5 B4
Nelson Rd. SS4	11 E2
Nelson Rd. SS9	21 E3
Nelson Rd. SS6	7 H3
Nelson St. SS1	5 B5
Ness Rd. SS3	24 D4
Nestuda Way. SS9	16 C5
Netherfield. SS7	13 F5
Nevada Rd. SS8	28 D2
Nevern Clo. SS6	7 H6
Nevern Rd. SS6	7 G6
New Park Rd. SS7	12 C4
New Rd. SS8	27 E7
New Rd. SS7	18 D3
New Rd. SS9	20 C5
Newell Av. SS3	25 G3
Newhall. SS4	10 D2
Newington Av. SS2	23 F2
Newington Clo. SS2	23 G2
Newlands Rd. SS8	28 D3
Newport Ct. SS6	6 D2
Newsum Gdns. SS6	6 C3
Newton Hall Gdns. SS4	10 D2
Newton Park Rd. SS7	13 G2
Nicholson Cres. SS7	13 H5
Nicholson Rd. SS7	13 G5
Nightingale Clo. SS2	17 E4
Nightingale Rd. SS8	28 D4
Nobles Green Clo. SS9	15 G3
Nobles Green Rd. SS9	15 G4
Nordland Rd. SS8	29 E3
Nore Rd. SS9	15 E2
Noredale. SS3	24 C5
Norfolk Av. SS9	20 D2
Norfolk Clo. SS8	28 A2
Norman Cres. SS4	7 G1
Normans Rd. SS8	28 D4
North Av. SS8	28 A4
North Av. SS2	5 C1
North Cres. SS2	16 D5
North Rd. SS0	22 B4
North Shoebury Rd. SS3	24 D1
North St. SS9	20 C5
North St. SS4	11 F6
Northern Av. SS7	12 C3
Northfalls Rd. SS8	29 F5
Northumberland Av. SS1	23 E5
Northumberland Cres. SS1	23 F5
Northview Dri. SS0	21 G4
Northville Rd. SS0	21 G1
Northwick Rd. SS8	27 B6
Norton Av. SS8	29 E4
Norwich Av. SS2	23 E1
Norwich Clo. SS2	23 E2
Norwich Cres. SS6	7 E1
Norwood Dri. SS7	26 E2
Nursery Clo. SS6	7 F5
Nutcombe Cres. SS4	11 E4
Oak Rd. SS8	28 C4
Oak Rd. SS4	11 E6
Oak Rd North. SS7	19 E3
Oak Rd South. SS7	19 E3
Oak Walk. SS5	9 E2
Oak Walky. SS7	12 B1
Oaken Grange Dri. SS2	1
Oakfield Clo. SS7	1
Oakfield Rd. SS7	1
Oakhurst Rd. SS6	
Oakhurst Rd. SS2	2
Oakleigh Av. SS1	2
Oakleigh Park Dri. SS9	2
Oakleighs. SS7	1
Oakley Av. SS6	
Oakwood Av. SS9	2
Oakwood Clo. SS7	2
Oakwood Rd. SS6	
Oastway. SS4	1
Oban Rd. SS2	2
Odessa Rd. SS8	2
Old Leigh Rd. SS9	2
Old Mead. SS2	1
Old Ship La. SS4	1
Old Southend Rd. SS1	
Olive Av. SS9	1
Olivia Dri. SS9	2
Orange Rd. SS8	2
Orchard Av. SS5	
Orchard Av. SS6	
Orchard Clo. SS5	
Orchard Gro. SS9	1
Orchard Mead. SS9	1
Orchard Side. SS7	1
Orchill Dri. SS7	1
Ormonde Av. SS8	1
Ormonde Av. SS4	
Ormonde Gdns. SS9	1
Ormsby Rd. SS8	2
Orrmo Rd. SS8	2
Orsett Av. SS9	1
Osborne Av. SS5	8
Osborne Rd. SS0	2
*Osprey Clo,	
Falcon Way. SS3	2
Ouida Rd. SS8	28
Oulton Av. SS8	2
Outing Clo. SS1	2
Overton Clo. SS7	1
Overton Dri. SS7	1
Overton Rd. SS7	1
Overton Way. SS7	1
Oxford Rd. SS8	28
Oxford Rd. SS4	1
Paarl Rd. SS8	28
Paddock Clo. SS9	15
Paignton Clo. SS6	
Pall Mall. SS9	20
Palmeira Av. SS0	22
Palmeira Par. SS0	22
Palmerston Rd. SS0	21
Palmerstone Rd. SS8	27
Pantile Av. SS. SS2	23
Papenburgh Rd. SS8	28
Pargat Dri. SS9	15
Park Av. SS8	29
Park Av. SS9	15
Park Chase. SS7	19
Park Cres. SS0	22
Park Gdns. SS5	9
Park La. SS8	29
Park La. Southchurch. SS1	23
Park La, Southend. SS1	5
Park Rd. SS8	29
Park Rd. SS9	20
Park Rd. SS1	5
Park Rd. SS7	13
Park St. SS1	5
Park Ter. SS0	
Park View Dri. SS9	19
Parkanaur Av. SS1	24
Parkfields. SS7	13
Parkgate. SS0	
Parklands Av. SS6	
Parklands. SS8	28
Parklands. SS4	10
Parkside. SS0	21
Parkstone Av. SS7	13
Parkstone Dri. SS2	13
Parkway. SS6	
Parkway Clo. SS9	

ons Lawn. SS3	24 C1	Prittle Clo. SS7	13 H4	Richmond St. SS2	23 F3	St Andrews Clo. SS8	27 D7
ons Rd. SS7	12 D1	Prittlewell Chase. SS0	22 A1	Ridgemount. SS7	13 E5	St Andrews Rd. SS4	11 E6
rdale. SS7	12 B2	Prittlewell Path. SS2	5 B1	Ridgeway. SS6	7 E5	St Andrews Rd. SS3	24 C5
ion Clo. SS2	23 F3	Prittlewell Sq. SS1	5 A5	Ridgeway Gdns. SS0	21 F5	St Anne's Rd. SS8	29 E5
ion Dri. SS9	20 D3	Prittlewell St. SS2	5 B3	Ringwood Dri. SS9	15 E4	St Anns Rd. SS2	5 B2
h Av. SS5	9 E2	Progress Rd. SS9	15 F5	Rivenhall. SS7	13 G1	St Augustines Av. SS1	24 A5
sons Av. SS6	7 E3	Prospect Clo. SS1	23 E5	River View Rd. SS7	26 D1	St Benets Rd. SS2	22 B1
tree Clo. SS2	23 E1	Puffin Pl. SS3	25 E2	Riverdale. SS9	15 G3	St Christophers Clo. SS8	27 D7
Trees. SS7	13 F4	Pulpits Clo. SS5	9 F2	Riviera Dri. SS1	23 E4	St Clare Meadow. SS4	11 F5
Av. SS3	25 G3	Purdeys Ind Est. SS4	17 G2	Roach Av. SS6	7 F6	St Clements Av. SS9	20 C3
am Rd. SS2	23 G3	Purdeys Way. SS4	17 H2	Roach Vale. SS6	16 A3	St Clements Clo. SS5	9 G5
bury Rd. SS0	21 G6	Purleigh Rd. SS6	6 D3	Roche Av. SS4	11 E6	St Clements Clo. SS7	12 C3
llestone. SS7	13 H5	Purley Way. SS2	16 D5	Rochefort Dri. SS4	17 F2	St Clements Cres. SS7	12 C3
urst Av. SS2	22 B2			Rochehall Way. SS4	17 H2	St Clements Dri. SS9	20 C2
ial Rd. SS8	28 B4	Quebec Av. SS1	5 C4	Rochester Dri. SS0	21 G1	St Clements Rd. SS7	12 C4
land Av. SS3	24 C5	Queen Annes Dri. SS0	21 G1	Rochester Mews. SS6	16 D6	St Davids Clo. SS9	19 G3
y Cottis Rd. SS4	11 F5	Queen Annes Mews. SS0	21 G1	Rocheway. SS4	11 G6	St Davids Ter. SS9	19 G3
y Rd. SS9	20 B3	Queen Elizabeth Chase.		Rochford Av. SS0	22 A3	St Davids Walk. SS8	27 D7
egrine Clo,		SS4	17 F3	Rochford Cnr. SS9	15 H4	St Edmunds Clo. SS2	23 E2
alcon Way. SS3	25 E2	Queens Av. SS9	20 D4	Rochford Garden Way.		St Georges Dri. SS0	22 A1
grine Dri. SS7	26 C1	Queens Rd. SS9	20 D5	SS4	11 E5	St Georges La. SS3	25 E5
y Rd. SS7	12 B6	Queens Rd. SS6	7 F5	Rochford Hall Clo. SS4	17 F2	St Georges Park Av. SS0	21 F4
orth Gdns. SS2	23 H3	Queens Rd. SS7	26 D1	Rochford Rd. SS8	28 D5	St Georges Wk. SS8	27 D7
orick Cres East. SS6	7 E3	Queensland Av. SS4	17 F3	Rochford Rd. SS2	17 E6	St Georges Wk. SS7	12 A2
rick Cres West. SS6	7 E3	Queensmere. SS7	13 H4	Rockall. SS9	16 B3	St Guiberts Rd. SS8	27 E6
mead Rd. SS7	26 B1	Queensway. SS2	5 A3	Rockleigh Av. SS9	21 E4	St Helens Rd. SS0	22 A4
ott Av. SS2	23 F2	Quorn Gdns. SS9	19 G4	Rodbridge Dri. SS1	23 H4	St James Av. SS1	24 B4
sso Way. SS3	25 G2	Quys La. SS4	17 F1	Roedean Clo. SS2	23 H3	St James Clo. SS8	27 D7
tts. SS8	27 D7			Roedean Gdns. SS2	23 H3	St James Clo. SS0	21 E2
tts Av. SS9	20 D1			Roggel Rd. SS8	28 D6	St James Gdns. SS0	21 F2
tts Clo. SS9	20 D1	Rackenford. SS3	24 D3	Roland La. SS8	28 B4	St James's Walk. SS5	8 D3
n Clo. SS6	7 G5	Rainbow Av. SS8	28 D4	Romanville Way. SS8	27 C8	St John's Cres. SS8	27 D7
n Gdns. SS6	7 G5	Rainbow Rd. SS8	28 D3	Romsey Clo. SS5	8 D3	St Johns Dri. SS6	6 B2
App. SS1	22 C5	Rampart St. SS3	25 F5	Romsey Cres. SS7	12 A3	St Johns Rd. SS7	13 H6
Hill. SS1	5 C5	Rampart Ter. SS3	25 F5	Romsey Dri. SS7	12 A3	St Johns Rd. SS0	22 A4
ims Clo. SS2	23 G3	Ramuz Dri. SS0	21 H4	Romsey Rd. SS7	12 A3	St Lawrence Gdns. SS9	15 H4
ims Way. SS7	19 F3	Randolph Clo. SS9	20 D2	Romsey Way. SS7	12 B3	St Leonards Rd. SS1	5 D4
Clo. SS8	27 E7	Randway. SS6	7 F5	Ronald Dri. SS6	6 D3	St Lukes Clo. SS8	27 D7
Clo. SS9	15 E5	Raphael Dri. SS3	25 F2	Ronald Hill Gro. SS9	20 B4	St Lukes Rd. SS2	5 D1
Rd. SS7	18 D3	Rat La. SS6	14 A3	Ronald Park Av. SS0	21 G4	St Marks Field. SS4	11 F6
trees. SS7	13 H5	Rattwick Dri. SS8	29 F4	Rookery Clo. SS6	7 E5	St Marks Rd. SS8	27 D7
wood Av. SS9	15 G5	Raven Dri. SS7	26 B1	Roosevel Av. SS8	28 B4	St Marks Rd. SS7	13 H6
ans Clo. SS1	5 B4	Ravendale Way. SS3	24 D1	Roots Hall Av. SS2	22 B2	St Martins Clo. SS6	7 E6
Newydd. SS1	23 G6	Ravenswood Chase. SS4	17 F3	Roots Hall Dri. SS2	22 B2	St Martins Clo. SS7	12 B2
Newydd Clo. SS1	23 G6	Rawreth Ind Est. SS6	4 D1	Rosary Gdns. SS0	21 F1	St Marys Clo. SS3	24 D2
sant Mews. SS1	5 D5	Rawreth La. SS6	7 E1	Rosbach Rd. SS8	28 D4	St Marys Clo. SS7	26 D2
sant Rd. SS1	5 D5	Ray Clo. SS8	28 B5	Rosberg Rd. SS8	29 E4	St Marys Dri. SS7	26 D2
hey Clo. SS1	23 H4	Ray Clo. SS9	20 A4	Rose Rd. SS8	28 B5	St Marys Rd. SS7	26 D3
mans. SS6	7 G2	Ray Walk. SS9	20 A4	Rose Way. SS4	17 H2	St Marys Rd. SS2	22 B2
berow Av. SS5	9 E2	Rayleigh Av. SS9	15 E3	Roseberry Av. SS7	12 C2	St Michaels Rd. SS8	27 D7
erow Ant Av. SS5	9 E2	Rayleigh Av. SS0	22 A3	Rosemead. SS7	12 C1	St Michaels Rd. SS7	14 C4
tree. SS1	24 B2	Rayleigh Downs Rd. SS6	14 D4	Roserna Rd. SS8	28 D5	St Pauls Rd. SS8	27 D7
t Clo. SS8	29 F5	Rayleigh Dri. SS9	20 C2	Rosewood La. SS3	25 E4	St Peters Rd. SS8	27 D7
t Rd. SS8	29 F5	Rayleigh Rd. SS9	15 E3	Rosslyn Clo. SS5	9 E2	St Peters Rd. SS5	8 B2
tead Clo. SS6	6 C4	Rayleigh Rd. SS7	13 H2	Rosslyn Rd. SS5	9 E2	St Vincents Rd. SS0	22 B5
rs La. SS7	19 E2	Rayleigh Spur Rd. SS6	6 A4	Rothchilds Av. SS6	7 E4	Sairard Clo. SS9	15 G4
rs La North. SS7	19 G1	Rayleigh Weir Ind Est.		Rothwell Clo. SS9	15 E5	Sairard Gdns. SS9	15 G4
es Walk. SS6	14 D1	SS7	14 A3	Round Hill Rd. SS7	18 B4	Salem Walk. SS6	6 D2
ar Rd. SS8	28 C5	Rayment Av. SS8	28 D5	Rowan Walk. SS9	15 G4	Salisbury Av. SS0	22 A3
ar Rd. SS6	7 H6	Raymonds Dri. SS7	13 E3	Royal Artillery Way. SS2	23 F1	Salisbury Rd. SS9	20 B3
ars Av. SS5	9 F5	Read Clo. SS7	9 G5	Royal Clo. SS4	10 D3	Salt Reach Clo. SS9	16 A6
oyfield Clo. SS9	15 G5	Recreation Av. SS9	20 D3	Royal Mews. SS1	5 B5	Samuels Dri. SS1	24 B2
ock Av. SS0	21 E1	Rectory Av. SS4	10 D3	Royal Ter. SS1	5 B5	San Remo Par. SS0	22 A5
land Av. SS1	5 C4	Rectory Clo. SS7	19 E3	Royer Clo. SS5	9 G5	San Remo Rd. SS8	29 E5
ers Way. SS2	17 G5	Rectory Garth. SS6	7 F4	Royston Av. SS2	22 D1	Sandbanks. SS7	18 D3
ings Av. SS2	23 F3	Rectory Gro. SS9	20 C5	Rubens Clo. SS3	25 F2	Sanderlings. SS7	12 C6
tens. SS6	7 E5	Rectory Rd. SS7	19 E3	Ruffles Clo. SS6	7 G3	Sanders Rd. SS8	28 B2
nters La. SS3	24 D1	Rectory Rd. SS5	10 A5	Runnymede Chase. SS7	13 F4	Sandhill Rd. SS9	15 E2
tice Clo. SS4	11 G6	Rectory Ter. SS5	9 G5	Runnymede Rd. SS8	28 B4	Sandhurst. SS8	27 C8
ton Gdns. SS6	7 F2	Redcliff Dri. SS9	20 D5	Runwell Ter. SS1	5 A5	Sandhurst Clo. SS9	20 D1
ton Rd. SS0	22 A5	Redstock Rd. SS2	5 B1	Runwood Rd. SS8	27 C7	Sandhurst Cres. SS9	20 D1
twood Clo. SS7	13 F2	Regency Clo. SS4	11 E6	Rush Clo. SS7	12 B3	Sandleigh Rd. SS9	21 E4
twood Dri. SS7	13 F2	Regency Grn. SS2	22 B2	Rushbottom La. SS7	12 B3	Sandon Clo. SS4	11 E5
rose Clo. SS8	28 B2	Regent Clo. SS9	6 D2	Ruskin Av. SS2	22 C2	Sandown Av. SS0	21 F3
ce Av. SS5	16 A5	Rembrandt Clo. SS3	25 G2	Ruskoi Rd. SS8	28 A3	Sandown Rd. SS7	13 G2
ce Av Nth. SS0	16 A5	Rembrandt Clo. SS8	28 B4	Russell Gro. SS4	11 H6	Sandpiper Clo. SS3	25 E2
ce Clo. SS2	16 D5	Repton Gro. SS2	16 B3	Russet Way. SS5	9 F1	Sandringham Av. SS5	8 D3
ce William Av. SS8	27 F5	Retreat Rd. SS8	9 E3	Rutherford Clo. SS8	15 E4	Sandringham Rd. SS1	23 F4
ces Av. SS7	13 F3	Retreat Rd. SS0	22 A5	Rutland Av. SS1	23 F4	Santour Rd. SS8	27 E6
ces St. SS1	5 A3	Rettendon Clo. SS6	6 D3	Rutland Gdns. SS4	10 D3	Satanita Rd. SS0	21 G5
cess Gdns. SS4	10 D3	Rhoda Rd. SS7	12 D4	Rydal Clo. SS6	7 G4	Saxon Clo. SS6	7 G1
cess Rd. SS7	7 H4	Rhoda Rd North. SS7	12 D4	Ryde Clo. SS6	15 E5	Saxon Gdns. SS3	24 C3
ry Av. SS2	22 B1	Richmond Av. SS0	22 A4	Rylands Rd. SS2	23 E2	Saxon Way. SS7	26 C2
ry Cres. SS2	22 B1	Richmond Av. SS6	12 B6			Saxonville. SS7	12 B4
ry View Rd. SS9	15 H6	Richmond Av. SS5	5 B5			Sayers. SS7	13 F2
rywood Cres. SS9	15 H5	Richmond Av. SS3	24 D4	Sackville Rd. SS2	23 G3	Scarborough Dri. SS9	20 D3
rywood Dri. SS9	15 H6	Richmond Dri. SS0	21 G1	Sadlers. SS7	12 A2	School La. SS7	26 D2
		Richmond Dri. SS6	7 F6	Saffory Clo. SS9	15 F3	School Way. SS9	20 D2
				St Agnes Dri. SS8	27 D7		

Street	Ref	Street	Ref	Street	Ref	Street	Ref
Paddocks. SS6	7 H4	Tower Ct Mews. SS0	22 B5	Villa Rd. SS7	12 B4	West Rd. SS0	22 A3
Parkway. SS8	28 B5	Towerfield Clo. SS3	25 E4	Village Dri. SS8	27 E7	West Rd. SS3	24 D4
Pavilions. SS0	22 B5	Towerfield Rd. SS3	25 E4	Village Hall Clo. SS8	27 D7	West St. SS9	20 C5
Ramparts. SS6	7 H5	Townfield Rd. SS4	11 G6	Villiers Way. SS7	13 F3	West St. SS4	17 F1
Redwoods. SS8	27 E7	Trafalgar Rd. SS3	24 D4	Vincent Clo. SS3	24 D4	West St. SS2	22 B1
Ridgeway. SS0	21 F5	Tree Lawn Dri. SS9	20 D1	Vincent Mews. SS3	24 D4	Westborough Rd. SS0	22 A3
Ridings. SS8	28 B2	Tree Lawn Gdns. SS9	21 E1	Virginia Clo. SS7	12 B2	Westbourne Clo. SS7	18 D1
Ridings. SS4	17 F1	Treecot Dri. SS9	21 E1	Voorburg Rd. SS8	29 E4	Westbourne Clo. SS5	9 G3
Rodings. SS9	15 G4	Trevia Av. SS8	28 C4	Voorne Av. SS8	28 D5	Westbourne Gro. SS0	21 F4
Rowlands. SS7	13 E5	Trinity Av. SS0	22 A5			Westbury. SS4	10 D4
Rundles. SS7	13 G3	Trinity Clo. SS6	7 G5	Waalwyk Dri. SS8	28 C3	Westbury Rd. SS2	23 E2
Russetts. SS4	10 D3	Trinity Rd. SS6	7 G5	Waarden Rd. SS8	28 B3	Westcliff Av. SS0	22 A5
Ryde. SS9	15 E5	Trinity Rd. SS2	23 E3	Waarem Av. SS8	28 B4	Westcliff Dri. SS9	20 B4
Saltings. SS7	I6 D3	Trinity Wood Rd. SS5	9 G1	Wakering Av. SS3	25 F4	Westcliff Gdns. SS8	29 F5
Sorrels. SS7	12 C2	Triton Way. SS7	13 G3	Wakering Rd. SS3	25 F3	Westcliff Par. SS0	22 A5
Spinnakers. SS7	12 B4	Truro Cres. SS6	7 F1	Wakering Rd. SS1	24 A1	Westcliff Park Dri. SS0	21 H4
Spinneys. SS5	8 D4	Tudor Clo. SS9	15 F3	Walk Ways. SS8	27 F6	Westerland Av. SS8	29 E4
Spinneys. SS9	15 H4	Tudor Clo. SS6	7 H5	Walker Dri. SS9	19 G4	Western Approaches. SS9	16 B3
Spinneys. SS6	14 D1	Tudor Clo. SS7	13 F4	Wall Rd. SS8	29 F4	Western Esplanade. SS8	28 C6
Terrace. SS3	25 E5	Tudor Gdns. SS9	20 B2	Wallace St. SS3	25 F4	Western Esplanade. SS1	5 A5
Terrace. SS7	26 D3	Tudor Gdns. SS3	24 C4	Wallis Av. SS2	22 B2	Western Rd. SS7	14 B4
Trunnions. SS4	17 G1	Tudor Rd. SS8	27 D8	Walnut Clo. SS5	9 E2	Western Rd. SS9	19 G5
Vintners. SS4	17 G5	Tudor Rd. SS9	15 F3	Walpole Walk. SS6	14 D1	Western Rd. SS6	6 D6
Weald. SS8	27 E7	Tudor Rd. SS0	22 B3	Walsingham Rd. SS2	22 D2	Westgate. SS3	25 E4
Westerings. SS5	9 E4	Tudor Way. SS5	9 F5	Walters Clo. SS9	15 H5	Westleigh Av. SS9	20 B3
Wheelwrights. SS2	17 G5	Tunbridge Rd. SS2	5 A1	Waltham Cres. SS2	22 D1	Westman Rd. SS8	29 F4
Willows. SS7	12 B4	Turner Clo. SS3	25 F2	Waltham Rd. SS6	6 D3	Westminster Dri. SS5	8 D3
Willows. SS1	24 A2	Twyzel Rd. SS8	28 D3	Walton Rd. SS1	23 H6	Westminster Dri. SS0	21 F4
Witterings. SS8	28 B2	Tylers Av. SS1	5 C4	Wambrook. SS3	24 C1	Weston Rd. SS1	5 B4
Woodlands. SS3	25 F3	Tylewood. SS7	13 H6	Wamburg Rd. SS8	29 E4	Westview Dri. SS6	6 D5
Woods. SS7	19 F2	Tylney Av. SS4	11 F5	Wansfell Gdns. SS1	23 H3	Westwater. SS7	12 B4
?r Clo. SS0	21 G1	Tyms Way. SS6	7 G3	Warberg Rd. SS8	29 E4	Westway. SS3	24 D5
?ma Av. SS8	28 B3	Tyrell Rd. SS7	26 B1	Warners Bri Chase. SS4	17 F4	Westwood Clo. SS7	13 H3
?balds Rd. SS9	20 B4	Tyrells. SS5	8 D4	Warners Gdns. SS4	17 F4	Westwood Gdns. SS7	18 D1
?len Rd. SS8	28 B3	Tyrone Rd. SS1	24 A4	Warren Chase. SS7	13 G4	Westwood Rd. SS8	28 B5
?d Av. SS8	27 E6	Tyrrel Dri. SS1	5 C3	Warren Clo.. SS8	7 E6	Wethersfield Clo. SS6	6 C3
?lmere Rd. SS7	13 E2	Ullswater Rd. SS7	12 D1	Warren Rd. SS9	19 G2	Weybourne Clo. SS2	22 D1
?selt Rd. SS8	28 B3	Ulster Av. SS3	24 C5	Warrior Sq. SS1	5 B4	Weybourne Gdns. SS2	22 D1
?tley Clo. SS9	21 E1	Undercliffe Gdns. SS9	20 D5	Warrior Sq East. SS1	5 C3	Weybridge Walk. SS3	24 D1
?mas Dri. SS8	27 E6	Underhill Rd. SS7	12 D5	Warrior Sq North. SS1	5 B3	Wheatley Clo. SS4	11 E4
?mpson Av. SS8	29 F4	Underwood Sq. SS9	20 B3	Warrior Sq Rd. SS3	25 E6	Whernside Av. SS8	28 D2
?ington Av. SS7	14 B4	Union La. SS4	11 F6	Warwick Clo. SS8	28 B2	Whistler Rise. SS3	25 F2
?ington Rd. SS6	14 D1	Upland Rd. SS9	21 E5	Warwick Clo. SS6	7 H5	White House Chase. SS6	7 G6
?rnbridge. SS7	12 B4	Uplands Clo. SS5	9 F4	Warwick Clo. SS7	12 C1	Whitefriars Cres. SS0	21 G6
?ndale. SS7	13 G2	Uplands Clo. SS7	12 B5	Warwick Dri. SS4	17 G3	Whitegate Rd. SS1	5 B4
?rndon Pk Clo. SS9	15 F6	Uplands Park Rd. SS6	7 F3	Warwick Gdns. SS6	7 H5	Whitehart Lane. SS5	9 F4
?rndon Pk Cres. SS9	15 E6	Uplands Rd. SS5	9 F4	Warwick Grn. SS6	14 D2	Whitehouse Meadows. SS9	16 B4
?rndon Pk Dri. SS9	19 H1	Uplands Rd. SS7	12 B5	Warwick Rd. SS6	7 G5	Whitehouse Rd. SS9	16 A4
?rney Bay Rd. SS8	28 A5	Upper Lambricks. SS6	7 G2	Warwick Rd. SS1	23 G6	Whiteways. SS8	28 D6
?rnford Gdns. SS2	17 F5	Upway. SS6	7 F3	Watchfield Dri. SS6	7 E6	Whiteways. SS9	16 A4
?rnhill. SS9	20 C1	Urmond Rd. SS8	28 B4	Waterdene. SS8	27 E5	Whittingham Av. SS2	23 G2
?rp Leas. SS8	28 C5			Waterford Rd. SS3	24 D5	Wick Chase. SS2	23 G3
?rpe Bay Gdns. SS1	24 A5	Vaagen Rd. SS8	28 B4	Waterhall. SS1	24 A2	Wickford Rd. SS0	22 A5
?rpe Clo. SS1	9 F5	Vadsoe Rd. SS8	28 B3	Waterloo Rd. SS3	24 D4	Wicklow Walk. SS3	24 C4
?rpe Esp. SS1	23 H6	Vale Av. SS2	5 B1	Watkins Way. SS3	25 E2	Wickmead Clo. SS2	23 G2
?rpe Gdns (Private).		Valance Clo. SS2	23 G2	Watlington Rd. SS7	12 B6	Willingale Av. SS6	6 D3
?5	9 F5	Valkyrie Rd. SS0	21 H5	Watson Clo. SS3	24 D3	Willingale Way. SS1	23 H3
?pe Hall Av. SS1	24 A2	Van Diemens Pass. SS8	29 F5	Watts La. SS4	17 F1	Willow Clo. SS8	28 A4
?pe Hall Clo. SS1	24 A2	Vanburg Rd. SS8	29 F5	Waverley Rd. SS7	12 C2	Willow Clo. SS6	15 H5
?rpe Rd. SS1	9 F5	Vanderwalt Av. SS8	29 E4	Wavertree Rd. SS7	12 B5	Willow Clo. SS5	10 A2
?pedene Gdns. SS3	24 D4	Vanguard Way. SS3	25 E3	Wayletts. SS9	15 E4	Willow Clo. SS6	7 F2
?dersley Church Rd.		Vardon Dri. SS9	19 G3	Weare Gifford. SS3	24 C2	Willow Dri. SS6	7 F2
?7	12 D3	Vaughan Av. SS2	23 F3	Weaverdale. SS3	24 D2	Willow Walk. SS7	18 D2
?dersley Gro. SS7	13 E4	Vaughan Clo. SS4	11 E3	Websters Way. SS6	7 F5	Willow Walk. SS6	9 F3
?dersley Park Rd.		Vaulx Rd. SS8	28 C3	Wedgwood. SS4	10 D2	Wilmarc Cres. SS6	7 E2
?7	12 C6	Venables Clo. SS8	28 D4	Weel Rd. SS8	29 E5	Wilmott Rd. SS2	16 D4
?low Dri. SS1	23 H4	Venlo Rd. SS8	28 C2	Weir Farm Rd. SS6	7 E6	Wilmslowe. SS8	29 E3
?lstone. SS7	13 H4	Ventham. SS8	27 F1	Weir Gdns. SS6	7 E5	Wilrich Av. SS8	29 E4
?rston Av. SS2	23 G3	Vermeer Cres. SS3	25 F3	Weir Pond Rd. SS4	11 F6	Wilson Rd. SS1	22 B5
?field Av. SS2	22 B2	Vernon Av. SS6	6 D3	Welbeck Av. SS6	6 D3	Wimborne Rd. SS2	5 C2
?urg Rd. SS8	28 A3	Vernon Rd. SS9	20 A4	Welbeck Clo. SS6	9 F4	Wimhurst Clo. SS6	9 E2
?ngham Way. SS6	6 D3	Viburg Rd. SS8	28 D5	Welbeck Rd. SS8	28 B5	Winbrook Clo. SS6	7 G6
?ers La. SS4	17 F2	Vicarage Clo. SS8	27 D8	Welch Clo. SS2	23 G2	Winbrook Rd. SS6	7 G6
?ern Av. SS0	21 G4	Vicarage Hill. SS7	26 D2	Wellingbury. SS7	12 C4	Winchester Clo. SS9	16 A3
?ers Field. SS7	13 E5	Vickers Rd. SS2	17 E4	Wellington Av. SS0	21 F4	Winchcombe Clo. SS9	20 C2
?ree Clo. SS9	20 D1	Victor Dri. SS9	20 D5	Wellington Rd. SS1	7 H3	Wincoat Clo. SS7	12 C6
?do Clo. SS1	5 C4	Victor Gdns. SS5	10 A3	Wells Av. SS2	16 D4	Wincoat Dri. SS7	12 B6
?do Rd. SS1	5 C4	Victoria Av. SS6	6 D2	Wellsfield. SS6	7 G2	Windermere Rd. SS3	5 D3
?ate. SS7	13 H3	Victoria Av. SS2	5 A1	Wellstead Gdns. SS0	21 F2	Windermere Rd. SS7	12 D1
?bridge Rd. SS5	9 F1	Victoria Circus. SS2	5 B3	Wendon Clo. SS4	10 D4	Windsor Clo. SS8	28 C5
?gres Rd. SS8	28 B3	Victoria Dri. SS9	20 C4	Wenham Dri. SS0	22 A2	Windsor Gdns. SS5	9 H5
?quay Clo. SS6	7 F2	Victoria Rd. SS3	25 H1	Wensley Rd. SS7	13 G4	Windsor Gdns. SS7	13 H4
?quay Dri. SS6	20 C4	Victoria Rd. SS9	20 D5	Wentworth Rd. SS2	22 C1	Windsor Rd. SS0	22 A4
?ington. SS3	24 D3	Victoria Rd. SS6	7 G3	Wesley Rd. SS1	5 D4	Windsor Way. SS6	7 G5
?si Rd. SS5	29 E5	Victoria Rd. SS1	23 E4	Wessem Rd. SS8	28 C2	Winsford Gdns. SS0	21 E1
?nan Clo. SS6	7 F6	Victory Path. SS0	21 F5	West Cres. SS8	27 F6		
?nan Cres. SS6	7 F6	Vikings Way. SS8	27 D7	West Grn. SS7	12 B3	Winter Gardens Path. SS7	26 E4
?can Clo. SS3	25 E2			West Point Pl. SS8	27 C7		

Street	Ref
Winterswyk Av. SS8	29 E4
Winton Av. SS0	22 A5
Withypool. SS3	24 C2
Wittem Rd. SS8	28 C2
Wood Av. SS5	9 E1
Wood End. SS5	9 E4
Wood Farm Clo. SS9	15 G6
Woodberry Clo. SS9	15 F6
Woodburn Clo. SS7	13 H4
Woodbury Clo. SS8	28 A2
Woodcote App. SS7	12 B2
Woodcote Rd. SS9	21 E3
Woodcote Way. SS7	12 B2
Woodcotes. SS3	25 E2
Woodcroft Clo. SS7	13 H5
Woodcutters Av. SS9	15 F6
Woodend Clo. SS7	13 H5
Woodfield Gdns. SS9	21 E5
Woodfield Pk Dri. SS9	21 E4
Woodfield Rd. SS9	21 E4
Woodfield Rd. SS7	19 F4
Woodgrange Clo. SS1	23 G4
Woodgrange Dri. SS1	23 E5
Woodham Pk Dri. SS2	26 C2
Woodham Rd. SS7	26 B1
Woodhurst Rd. SS8	27 E8
Woodland Clo. SS7	19 G2
Woodlands Av. SS6	7 G6
Woodlands Clo. SS5	8 D4
Woodlands Clo. SS6	7 F6
Woodlands Park. SS9	19 G2
Woodlands Rd. SS5	8 D4
Woodleigh. SS9	19 G4
Woodleigh Av. SS9	20 C2
Woodley Walk. SS3	25 E1
Woodlow. SS7	13 G2
Woodpond Av. SS5	9 E4
Woodside. SS9	15 E5
Woodside Av. SS7	12 B1
Woodside Chase. SS5	9 F5
Woodside Clo. SS9	15 E5
Woodside Rd. SS5	8 B4
Woodside View. SS7	12 C1
Woodstock Cres. SS5	8 D3
Woodville Clo. SS4	11 E5
Woodville Rd. SS8	29 E4
Woolpack. SS3	24 C3
Worcester Dri. SS6	7 H6
Wordsworth Clo. SS2	22 D2
Wren Av. SS9	15 F3
Wren Clo. SS7	12 A2
Wren Clo. SS9	15 F3
Wroxham Clo. SS9	15 E5
Wyatts Dri. SS1	23 G5
Wyburn Rd. SS7	14 B5
Wyburns Av. SS6	7 G6
Wyburns Av West. SS6	14 B3
Wycombe Av. SS7	12 A3
Yamburg Rd. SS8	29 E4
Yarnacott. SS3	24 C3

Street	Ref
Yeovil Chase. SS0	21 F1
York Clo. SS8	28 B2
York Clo. SS6	14 D2
York Rise. SS6	14 D2
York Road. SS4	10 D1
York Road. SS6	14 D2
York Road. SS1	5 C4
Young Clo. SS9	16 B4
Zandi Rd. SS8	28 D6
Zealand Dri. SS8	29 F5
Zelham Dri. SS8	29 G5
Zider Pass. SS8	29 G5
Zuidorp Rd. SS8	29 E4

CANEWDON

Street	Ref
Althorne Way. SS4	30 C4
Anchor La. SS4	30 A5
Birch Clo. SS4	30 B5
Butts Paddock. SS4	30 A4
Canewdon Hall Clo. SS4	30 A4
Canute Clo. SS4	30 B4
Chestnut Path. SS4	30 B5
Church Grn. SS4	30 B4
Docketts Mead. SS4	30 B4
Gardeners La. SS4	30 B5
High St. SS4	30 B4
Lambourne Hall Rd. SS4	30 B4
Lark Hill Rd. SS4	30 A5
Rowan Way. SS4	30 B5
Scotts Hall Rd. SS4	30 A5
Sycamore Way. SS4	30 A4
Willow Walk. SS4	30 B5

GREAT WAKERING

Street	Ref
Alexandra Rd. SS3	4 B2
Barrow Hall Rd. SS3	4 A1
Beach Ct. SS3	4 E3
Bell Ho. SS3	4 C2
Bray Clo. SS3	4 A4
Bridge Rd. SS3	4 F2
Brookside Av. SS3	4 E3
Broomways. SS3	4 E3
Brougham Clo. SS3	4 B2
Caversham Av. SS3	4 A4
Chapel La. SS3	4 D2
Cherrytree Chase. SS3	4 E4
Churchfields. SS3	4 A4
Common Rd. SS3	4 D2
Conway Av. SS3	4 C2
Cookham Ct. SS3	4 A4

Street	Ref
Coronation Clo. SS3	4 B2
Crouchmans Av. SS3	4 C2
Cupids Chase. SS3	4 E4
Estuary Gdns. SS3	4 E3
Exhibition La. SS3	4 B2
Fairfield. SS3	4 C2
Frobisher Way. SS3	4 A4
Glebe Clo. SS3	4 E2
Goldsworthy Dri. SS3	4 E4
Havengore Clo. SS3	4 E3
Havenside. SS3	4 A1
Havering Clo. SS3	4 D2
High St. SS3	4 B2
Home Farm Clo. SS3	4 D2
INDUSTRIAL ESTATES:	
Star La Ind Est. SS3	4 B2
Kingston Av. SS3	4 A4
Lee Lotts. SS3	4 C2
Lindsey Rd. SS3	4 D2
Little Wakering Hall La. SS3	4 C2
Little Wakering Rd. SS3	4 A1
Maitland Pl. SS3	4 A4
Mariners Ct. SS3	4 E3
Mercer Av. SS3	4 C2
Montgomery Ct. SS3	4 A4
Moreland Clo. SS3	4 C2
Morris Chase. SS3	4 F3
Morris Clo. SS3	4 F3
Mountbatten Dri. SS3	4 A4
New England Cres. SS3	4 E3
New Rd. SS3	4 D2
Newstead Rd. SS3	4 D2
North St. SS3	4 D2
Northfield Cres. SS3	4 C2
Old Hall Ct. SS3	4 C2
Old School Meadow. SS3	4 A2
Olivers Cres. SS3	4 C2
Orchard Clo. SS3	4 C2
Poynters Chase. SS3	4 E4
Pounters La. SS3	4 A4
Roding Clo. SS3	4 D2
Rushley Clo. SS3	4 C2
St Johns Clo. SS3	4 D2
St Johns Rd. SS3	4 D2
Seaview Dri. SS3	4 D3
Shoebury Rd. SS3	4 D3
Southend Rd. SS3	4 A2
Star La. SS3	4 A2
Star La Ind Est. SS3	4 B2
Stuart Clo. SS3	4 B2
Sunbury Ct. SS3	4 A4
Suttons Rd. SS3	4 E4
The Anchorage. SS3	4 D2
The Cedars. SS3	4 D2
The Crofts. SS3	4 A1
Townfield Walk. SS3	4 A2
Twyford Av. SS3	4 C2
Victoria Dri. SS3	4 E4
White Hall Rd. SS3	4 D2
Woodley Walk. SS3	4 A4

HULLBRIDGE

Abbey Clo. SS5
Abbey Rd. SS5
Alfreda Av. SS5
Ambleside Gdns. SS5
Ashdene Clo. SS5
Beech Rd. SS5
Birchdale. SS5
Broom Rd. SS5
Burnham Rd. SS5
Cedar Dri. SS5
Central Av. SS5
Cherry Dene Clo. SS5
Coventry Clo. SS5
Coventry Hill. SS5
Creek Vw. SS5
Crouch Av. SS5
Crouch Meadows. SS5
Crouch View Gro. SS5
Elm Gro. SS5
Esplanade. SS5
Ferry Rd. SS5
Grasmere Av. SS5
Harrison Gdns. SS5
Highelms Rd. SS5
Hillcrest Av. SS5
Hilltop Av. SS5
Kendal Clo. SS5
Keswick Av. SS5
Long La. SS5
Lower Rd. SS5
Malyons La. SS5
Mapledene Av. SS5
Mayfield Av. SS5
Meadow Rd. SS5
Monksford Dri. SS5
Oakleigh Rd. SS5
Padgetts Way. SS5
Pinewood Clo. SS5
Pooles La. SS5
Promenade. SS5
River View Gdns. SS5
Rydal Clo. SS5
South Vw. SS5
The Avenue. SS5
The Drive. SS5
The Priories. SS5
The Walk. SS5
Thorpedene Av. SS5
Tyndale. SS5
Wallace Clo. SS5
Watery La. SS5
Waxwell Rd. SS5
West Av. SS5
Windermere Av. SS5